Doing things that Matter

Doing things that Matter

DREAM WILDLY

LIVE DIFFERENTLY

LOVE RECKLESSLY

LEAD COURAGEOUSLY

TIM MANNIN

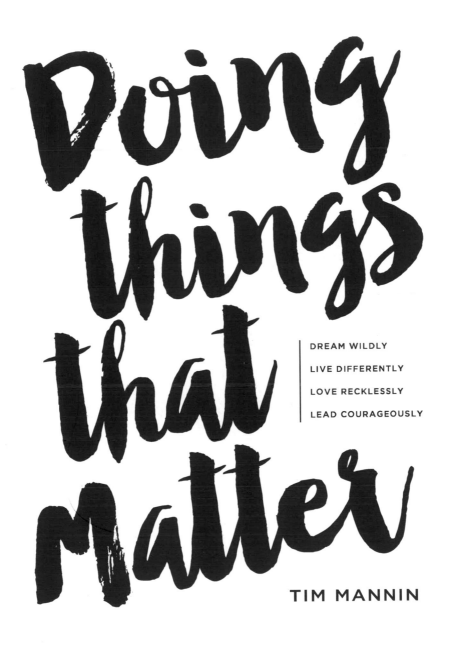

UPTOWN
PUBLISHING

Uptown Publishing
421 Northwest 23rd Street | Oklahoma City, Oklahoma 73103 USA
www.doingthingsthatmatter.com

Book design copyright © 2017 by Hazel Paper Co, LLC. All rights reserved.
Cover design by Leslie Koch | Hazel Paper Co. | www.hazelpaperco.com

Published in the United States of America

ISBN: 978-0692984864
1.Religion / Christian Life / Spiritual Growth
2. Religion / Christian Church / Leadership

To Christie,
the love of my life and best friend,
thank you for never settling for normal.

To Emily, Carys, Addi, and Greyson,
God has set you apart for a special work.

CONTENTS

AUTHOR'S NOTE

It was in early 2012 that I began writing this book. It was about 25,000 words longer than it is now (I was a little long-winded at first). It took longer to finish than expected and went through many revisions before anyone ever read it, with the exception of my wife and mom of course. My hope is that the words that remain are words that *matter*.

There are many reasons why the journey of writing this book took longer than expected. During that span of time, my wife, Christie, and I had our fourth child (new kids sort of slow things down, but in a good way). We also experienced God leading our hearts in deeper ways than ever before. Those things led Christie and I into a calling to plant a new church in the heart of Oklahoma City.

At the beginning of 2013, we planted Oklahoma City Community Church, and that has changed everything, including this book. We also moved to a new home (well, it was an old house that we had to renovate and make feel new again), started our kids in a new school, and bought a mini van. So we were up to a few things to say the least.

I believe all that has happened has helped the book. I have a simple hope and prayer for you. I pray that as you read this book, God's Spirit stirs something fresh in you and that what you read helps you as you follow Jesus. That's my prayer and hope.

NOTE TO MENTORS, MINISTRY LEADERS, AND GROUP LEADERS

If you are a mentor, ministry leader, or group leader let me begin by thanking you for reading this book. While writing, I always dreamed the book would be used as a resource to help mentors and leaders, like yourself, to disciple others. This book has largely been influenced and informed from conversations I've had with friends, mentors, peers, and students. *Conversations* are a big part of our lives. I've written with a hope that each chapter will create further conversations. Utilize the questions at the end of each chapter to push conversations deeper. Thank you for the investment you are making in others. I pray this book serves your cause well.

BEFORE THE PARTS

CHAPTER ONE

The Silent Beckoning

This is a book about life.
A few years back, a random thought crossed my mind and took my heart by storm.

The thought was a question.

What am I doing?

The question wasn't about what I was actually doing in that moment.

No, it was more like, "What. Am. I. Doing?"

I wrestled with this question while I carried on with my everyday job and routine that filled up the best hours of my day. Nothing was bad about what I did every day, and in many ways, it had absolutely nothing to do with the question. What created unrest in my soul was more of a feeling that something was missing in my life. This certainly influenced my thoughts about things like my job but more importantly, it affected the way I felt about nearly everything.

That question led to many more questions. And those questions led to others.

I had to start answering all these questions about my life because the alternative was to avoid them and to simply keep plugging away at the life that seemed to be missing something. If one dares to truly consider the "What am I doing?" question, it will place everything on the line. Jobs are questioned, passions and priorities are reassessed, and we wonder what really matters in this life?

Is having a successful job the only thing that matters? Or is it all about having a job I love and am passionate about? Do I have to do something in a third world country to feel like my life matters? Is the gospel the *only* thing that matters? And does that mean that I should focus all my energy on trying and reach people for Christ? What about a healthy family life and marriage—that matters too, right? Does everything matter? Does anything matter?

Like I said, one question led to another.

Most days I have the privilege of taking my kids to school. It has become special time to start our day. Even the kids seem to appreciate the value of this short time together. As we approach their quaint, classic 1920s school building that sits in the heart of our city, we finish our time by saying the same thing together every day.

I say, "Okay, remember…today *do something that*"—and they fill in the last word in unison, saying—"*matters!*"

That is the last thing we say to one another as they head into their everyday *life*.

Our family first talked about doing things that matter when my two oldest daughters were eight and five years old. I began by asking them if they knew what it meant to shine God's light, and I received a couple of blank stares in return. I explained that a kindergartener and a third grader could shine God's light by sharing with friends, saying kind words, being encouraging, giving away treats, being a good friend, making friends with the kids who don't have many, talking about the good things of God when you can, and being respectful and thankful to your teachers. We agreed that these types of things mattered and by doing them, we could show people who God is. Perhaps this simple, childlike understanding is a place to begin for all of us.

After we say our *do things that matter* statement together, I watch my kids walk into their school, and I have a hopeful, and possibly, overly idealistic anticipation of them making a radical impact. As I leave and head towards my everyday life I wonder, "What am I going to do today that matters?"

꙳.꙳.꙳

This brings me to Mt. Everest.

Some of my favorite television shows are reality shows that share or even reenact stories of people who overcome extreme circumstances in order to survive unlikely peril. In other words, I love stories about people snatching life from the jaws of death. I guess I enjoy these because they are so different from my normal life. Let's just say that I am more of a *city boy,* and I enjoy my Starbucks and MacBook Pro more than a crisp adventure in God's wilderness (where most of those stories take place).

A few years ago, I watched a full season of a show called *Everest.* Mt. Everest is the pinnacle for testing human survival. Over the years I've had a semifascination with the stories that surround this beastly mountain. The show was dedicated to the brave and absolutely crazy people who attempt to climb to the summit of Mt. Everest. Standing on the top of Mt. Everest at over 29,000 feet in the air has to be one of the most exhilarating feelings a person can experience.

I love how adventurer Bear Grylls described it during his climb to the top, "Technology can put a man on the moon, but only a person's spirit can put someone up here."[1]

The peak of Everest may be the most exclusive piece of land on planet earth.

To literally stand on top of the world would be an incredible experience, but the hardships these climbers must endure is nearly insurmountable. The show chronicled teams of climbers struggling to overcome the brutal conditions. They endured temperatures of fifty degrees below zero and oxygen levels that are approximatcly a third of what's available at sea level. As of the writing of this book, about four thousand different climbers have made it to the summit of Everest with some having done it multiple times, and most having paid some physical price for the ascent.

Two times per year, there is a short window of only a few short weeks where the conditions even allow people to be on the mountain. Most of the year, the conditions are too brutal and the winds are too strong. The jet stream would literally blow a person off the mountain that dared to climb it at the wrong time; however during these few weeks a year, the warm monsoon air blows across the Himalayas, the winds simmer just enough, and a short glimmer of possibility is provided.

Climbers call this the *silent beckoning* of Everest.

The moment when the weather breaks and the mountain calls, it beckons the climber to come. The timetable is always a bit unknown, but if a climber wants a shot at Everest, that would be their chance.

Near the top of the summit in what is known as the death zone (above 26,000 feet), over two hundred climbers have perished. Dozens of their bodies remain frozen in the snow because nothing can be done about it. The bodies can't be taken out by helicopter because the air is too thin, and they can't be carried down because it's too dangerous. What? Crazy.

So while they journey to the summit, climbers pass by and see their predecessors who died doing the very thing they are doing. For those strong enough to survive the ascent nearly 90 percent of the climbers will experience frostbite with the likely potential to lose fingers, toes, or worse.

The most fascinating part of the show was the interviews with the climbers at the end of the season.

Each climber was asked, "Was it worth it?"

Without flinching, every one of the climbers with tearful eyes, nubs for hands, and skin-grafted noses, assured the audience that every challenging step was worth it. Nearly all of them went as far as to say they would do it all again. (Uhhh, did they notice that they are missing an ear?)

The commitment and physical sacrifice is inspiring, to say the least. I believe that willingness to sacrifice anything is what has always fascinated me about Everest and those brave enough to respond to the silent beckoning.

What if your life embodied this sort of dedication? What if your summit was becoming everything God created you to be?

Imagine living with an unwavering focus on the destination regardless of the outcome and what may be sacrificed along the way.

A life like that could create a movement.

A movement like that that could change the world.

On the heels of that random question of *what am I doing*, and in the midst of telling my children to *do things that matter*, a silent beckoning was bidding my wife, Christie, and I to come. At first, we weren't sure what this silent beckoning was, but we couldn't ignore it any longer. We were so tired of the mediocre existence we were living. We realized we weren't living a life that had anything movement-worthy or even story-worthy. We wanted more for our life.

One of the most quoted verses in the Bible happens to be about life.

Jesus says in John 10:10 (NIV), "The thief comes only to steal and kill and destroy; I have come that they may have life, and have it to the full."

When Jesus claimed that he had come to give us life to the full, or as it says in the King James Version, "To have life more abundantly," he is speaking about more than just our eternal inheritance (which would be enough!). He is also speaking about our everyday life.

The Greek phrase used for having life more abundantly means to have a *superabundance* of life.[2] A superabundance of life sounds like a pretty fantastic thing.

John 10:10 can't be interpreted with the assumption that Jesus is promising some sort of physical or material improvement in life. (This would trivialize the meaning of what is being said). Instead this is a promise that a life with Jesus is a life that is *full* of *life*.

The opposite of life is death. I don't think any of us want a life full of death—no, we want a life full of life; however, we let death creep in and steal life from us all the time. We allow fear to stop us (life stolen by death). We believe the lie that we aren't good enough (life stolen by death). We settle for status quo (life stolen by death). We allow busyness to control us (life stolen by death). We give up on someone (life stolen by death). We quit dreaming (life stolen by death).

Let's not forget what Jesus said first in this verse, "the thief comes only to steal and kill and destroy…" You and I have an enemy in this life that is out to destroy our lives. He is out to deceive us and steal our life right out from under us. The enemy (aka the devil, Satan, Lucifer, the evil one) hates you. As real as there is a God in heaven who loves you without end, there is an enemy that hates everything about you and is determined to destroy your life, one small deception at a time.

When Carys, our middle daughter, was five years old she asked a startling question. Our family was in the kitchen getting ready for dinner when an off-the-cuff comment was made about Satan (you know, normal conversation), and Carys innocently cut into the conversation with a machete.

"Who is Satan?" she asked (nothing like casual dinner conversation at the Mannin house).

It was a beautiful and terrible moment.

It was beautiful because she didn't know who he was. She was too innocent and precious. It was terrible because I would have to tell her, and she would come to understand who he really is in the future. I told her that Satan was God's enemy and that he was trying to hurt every good thing that God has done and is doing.

Emily, our oldest, chimed in and said, "Yeah, and he lives down there!" as she pointed to the ground emphatically.

Satan is out to destroy you and steal every good thing that God has done and is doing. He will deceive you by telling you that you aren't good enough or that you've made too many mistakes. You will be paralyzed by fears. You will be told to think more realistically. He'll try to shatter your self-esteem. You will be told that you have good reasons and excuses to give up. You will be distracted and think too much about money, success, the size of your home, and the brand of car you drive. You will be overwhelmed by a busy lifestyle to mask the reality that you aren't doing anything that really matters. The thief will try to deceive you to believe that life has nothing more to offer.

Jesus is saying I have come to *snatch life from the jaws of death!*

Now Jesus was quick to say that life would not be an easy endeavor. Jesus shares a difficult truth about this in his Sermon on the Mount.

> Enter through the narrow gate. For wide is the gate and broad is the road that leads to destruction and many enter through it. But small is the gate and narrow is the road that leads to life, and only a few find it. (Matthew 7:13-14, NIV)

I love how Eugene Peterson paraphrases this passage in The Message.

> Don't look for shortcuts to God. The market is flooded with surefire, easygoing formulas for a successful life that can be practiced in your spare time. Don't fall for that stuff, even though crowds of people do. The way to life—to God—is vigorous and requires total attention. (Matthew 7:13–14, The Message)

Jesus declares that the pathway to God and the road to the *life* we all seek will be narrow, and it will require our total attention. He also states that most of us are *not on that road.* Many in this world choose roads that are easy and appear to be low-risk endeavors. Jesus clearly states in Matthew 7 that if we want to be on the road that leads to real life, it will require relentless attention, sacrifice, and passion. Some may want to chime in here and point out that this passage is about *eternal life* and not necessarily about life in the here and now.

To that thought I would ask, "When and where does eternity begin and end?"

Eternity has begun, and Jesus has invited us to enter the narrow way that leads to *life*.

Most of us attach ourselves to what we've always known. It's just the way most of us operate. We don't change careers because we wonder what will happen if we do something new and fail. We don't radically speak into our family dysfunction because it's the way it has always been. We don't change the status quo, dream new dreams, or turn the apple cart over because it's easier to stay with what we already know.

Aren't you tired of the worn-out rambling and conversations about who and what we should be, and aren't you ready to *do it* and *be it*.

No matter what changes are necessary?

I am probably like many of you. You see I am a United States citizen, and I would be classified as middle class. My wife's name is Christie, and she is a beautiful, talented, and amazing woman who can cook something fierce and can sing lights out. We have four incredible kids—Emily, Carys, Addison, and Greyson. I love sports, bonsai trees, and mini corn dogs.

You may be thinking, "That's not like me."

You're right. That's not why we are alike.

We are alike because we are all struggling to figure life out. Our nationality, race, age, socioeconomics, family, history, and interests are all important to the person we are today; however, what unites us is a common pursuit of life to the full. You and I aren't that different. I know this because the human quest to experience the fullness of life has been happening for centuries.

God's word is littered with people who have walked before us with this same pursuit.

So we are alike.

We are humans. We share more in common than we have differences. The hope that exists within these pages is that we can explore some of the questions, hopes, dreams, and purposes of our humanity. This book invites you to consider your life and the path you are choosing every day.

Because maybe it can be better. Better for others around you. Better for your family. Better for your career. Better for the glory of God. Better for you.

Are you choosing the path *to life—to God,* or is life simply choosing you? Has whatever life brought you become your reality? Does your life feel more like you are keeping up with life's demands rather than experiencing fullness? I have found myself going through the motions of a life that has been handed to me, instead of living the life I was created to live.

What if you attempted to reframe, rethink, or even *reimagine they way you do life?* Chances are your faith needs you to ask yourself new questions and to act on new discoveries. As you read through this book, you will be introduced to four values, which are the undercurrent to a life of *doing things that matter.*

While writing this book, Christie and I were in a conversation about *life,* which has become one of the most important conversations we've ever had. She said something I will never forget.

She said, "I'm tired of talking about the life we ought to be living while sitting here and letting that life pass us by. We need to get off our butts and go after it."

That simple conversation set us on a course of seeking the Lord like never before, trusting him in ways we never imagined, and discovering massive things about *who* he wanted us to *be.*

Becoming people who dream wildly, live differently, love recklessly, and lead courageously is the journey we find ourselves on.

You've probably heard someone say something to the effect, "If you want to know what someone believes, simply observe his or her daily life."

Christie and I have learned that we can't just say these types of things, we actually have to live it by embodying the things God has called us to.

Does your daily life represent what you say you believe?

Every day when my kids walk into their school I am hopeful that encouraging them to do things that matter will end up mattering. Occasionally, they will share a story with Christie and me about how they gave to a friend, said a kind word, or choose to help a classmate in need. They share the story and immediately connect it with doing things that matter. It's actually working.

About six months after we began saying this with our kids every morning, Emily came home from school and had some questions for us. She shared with us that she had been having conversations with a friend for several weeks on the bus ride home about God and the Bible. Her friend had told Emily that her parents didn't believe in God, but she was curious about God anyway. So on her own, Emily had taken her Bible in her backpack and started reading her stories from the Bible on the way home from school. She finally involved us because she had told her friend all the stories she knew, and she needed our help so she could share more stories.

What? We had no clue she had been doing this (so yes, this was a very proud parent moment). We gave her one of those kid's books full of Bible stories to take in her backpack, and she continued to read them to her friend every day on the bus ride home.

A few days later she asked Christie and I, "What do I do if she wants to invite Jesus into her life?"

Who is this kid?

No wonder Jesus spoke of the pure faith of children. Christie and I decided that this was pure and innocent, and we wanted to keep it that way and not muddy it up with too much complexity.

We told Emily that all that she needed to do was ask her friend if she believed in God and wanted to have a relationship with Jesus, and if her friend said yes, they could pray together, and she could ask Jesus to come into her life. We tried to make it simple, knowing that God is bigger than any right process. We trusted God's presence would be with these two children if the precious moment presented itself.

The very next day, Emily came running through the door beaming with excitement and unpacked the story of how she helped her friend invite Christ into her life on the bus ride home. She told us about how she asked her friend if she believed in God, how she helped her understand what a relationship with Jesus is, and how she helped her to pray and ask Jesus into her heart. As she emphatically told us this story she looked at us and asked, "That's doing things that matter, right?"

Uhh, yes, Emily, I think you are getting it (maybe more than I am getting it).

> Doing things that matter
> don't happen by accident.
> They happen on purpose.

A story led to those moments for my daughter to do the brave things that God put in front of her on that school bus. Becoming a person who writes a story of doing things that matter will likely be preceded by the moment when you look at yourself in the mirror, or you look at your spouse, or at your best friend and say something like, "I'm tired of talking about the life I ought to be living and letting life pass me by. It's time to get off my butt and go after it."

Every dream, every worthy endeavor, and every movement begins with discontent, frustration, compassion, hunger, desperation, or pain.

You may feel one of those things, or you may be feeling all of them—each of them represents an emptiness that needs to be filled. It's the silent beckoning of life bidding you to come—to do something that matters!

Discontent can eventually turn into action. Frustration will give way to a dream. Compassion can turn into service. The hungry eventually eat. Desperation will take us to our knees. Pain will refine us.

The life that Jesus talked about in John 10:10 and the one he described in Matthew 7 as a narrow path that few take, that life is silently beckoning all of us to come. It's bidding us to step into new, unfamiliar, and faithful places. All who go to this place emphatically say, "It was worth it."

The four parts of the book will not only serve as the framework of the book, but it will also create a foundation to a life of doing things that matter. Becoming a person who dreams wildly, lives differently, loves recklessly, and leads courageously for the sake of the gospel leads to a *life* of stories that matter.

So this is a book about life.

Your Life.

⁂

Questions for Reflection And Conversation

1. Does John 10:10 encourage you? How does it remind you of the battle that we face in this life?

2. How does Matthew 7:13–14 speak to your heart? Do you look for shortcuts? Is your pursuit of life or God vigorous? Why or why not?

3. Does your daily life represent what you say you believe? If so, how? If not, what challenges are you facing?

4. Do you feel a sort of *silent beckoning* within your life, something bidding you to come? Describe.

How life is stolen by death:
1. Fear
2. Believe I am not good enough.
3. Settle for the status quo.
4. Allow busyness to control my life.
5. Give up on someone
6. Quit dreaming.
7. Be distracted about:
   a) money
   b.) success
   c.) size of house
   d.) brand of car
   e.) clothing
   f.) friends
   g.) family
   h.)

THE FIRST PART

DREAM WILDLY

What if we allowed the impossible to become possible?

CHAPTER TWO

Becoming a Dreamer

Right after I turned thirty years old, I went to see my doc-tor who thankfully is a friend of mine. I hadn't seen him in some time, so we had a long conversation to catch up and talk about life. The conversation eventually turned to him inquiring about my activity and overall physical and spiritual health. He empathized with my busy life of being a pastor, having three chil-dren all under the age of seven (at the time), and the number of other excuses I had for not having healthy habits.

Then he said something that pierced me in the *gut.*

He said, "Well, I see you've put on some weight."

This moment definitely pricked my ego. I had always felt like I had maintained a good weight. I hadn't put on the twenty pounds in the first year of marriage like everyone predicted; however, admittedly in my late twenties, my waist size was slightly increas-ing, I had just thought no one else was noticing.

I had finally put on that twenty pounds (and maybe a lit-tle more) that everyone had predicted, and my secret was now exposed sitting in my doctor's office. I wasn't out of control, but he wanted to help me before it got any worse. It was painful but utterly freeing to have someone talk to me about the disciplines I had to adopt in my life in order to be healthy physically and spiritually. But here's what I loved about what he did and what I hope you really hear in this book. He didn't tell me exactly *what to do.* I didn't walk out of his office with a new checklist of what it means to live a healthy life.

He simply called it like it was, encouraged me, provided me with some wisdom, and then as we wrapped up the conversation, he said a statement that has become a rallying cry in my life.

"You only have one life to live and no one is responsible for it but you."

That thought is pretty sobering.

It's obvious, but it pulls everything into focus very quickly.

That experience in my doctor's office inspired something deep in me. I had to go home and start talking with Christie about where we were headed with our family. We had discussions about physical health and even longer discussions about our spiritual health. It eventually led to conversations about what the heck we were doing with our lives.

Since 1998, Christie and I have been serving and working in church ministry. Over the years, I've been a youth pastor, worship leader, video director, executive pastor, intern, grill master, college pastor, wedding planner, church planter, event director, graphic artist, speaker, interior decorator, stagehand, and a few other random things—not necessarily in that order, but every part of the hilariously random journey of being in ministry has mattered. Every part of our story was a significant season of learning, and each has contributed to Christie and me submitting to the biggest call of our life thus far.

In 2012, God called us to plant a church in Oklahoma City. OKC is our home city, and we experienced an unquestionable call to contribute to the work being done for the kingdom in an urban area within the heart of the city that has long been gospel deficient. So in November 2012, Oklahoma City Community Church was born with our first core group gatherings. On Easter of 2013 we began having weekly services.

Early on, Christie and I decided to pray that God would stir people's hearts to be a part of the church with us. God led us to be dedicated to prayer and to telling our story instead of going on a recruitment campaign. We didn't want to convince people to do this, rather in the beginning, we wanted people to come with us who felt compelled to be a part of it (whoever that may be). We wanted God to design the community. We began praying for a team who would be clueless enough (I mean spiritual enough) to jump in neck-deep with us. We felt like we had a story to tell about what God was doing in us, but we didn't have any money to offer, perks of the job, or even a guaranteed group of people to meet and have a church with. All we had was a promise that whoever God called to be a part of the church plant team with us would get hang out with our family—a lot!

We had no clue who God would stir and eventually call to join our team. By the time we actually started our church, we saw five people join our church planting team, four of them left full-time ministry jobs to join our unpaid adventure of seeing what would happen. What's amazing is that the Spirit recruited each one of them on their own, we didn't have to recruit a team. All we did was tell our story. We can honestly say God brought the perfect people into this journey with us. Even though as I write this we are still at the beginning of this church planting adventure, Christie and I look back and can't ever thank our friends Ryan Moore, Courtney Whittier, Jessica Cox, Jamie and Carrie Stolp, and Stephen and Jenny Thorne enough for stepping out with us in those early days. In many ways they exercised a faith and trust that I can't comprehend. We are forever grateful to them. We strongly felt that he told us to simply pray, tell our story, and wait for him to draw people, and that's what he actually did! We didn't build a team. God united hearts and created a community.

Since those beginning days, others beyond that initial team have been stirred as well. We had many join our initial core group and now our growing church. Some old friends, many new friends, and even our parents (what a blessing to have family with us) are on this church planting journey with us. We are witnessing God do a work within us that feels genuine, pure, and most importantly, it's about Him and His Church. We try and not take ourselves too seriously. We certainly take the role and responsibility of the Church in this world crazy serious, but we realize our church isn't always going to be the most important thing in everyone's schedule, and we aren't going to be the coolest or greatest church to ever exist. Even when we named our church, we decided to intentionally steer away from a cute or trendy name, or even a name with a hidden theological message. We felt our name needed to communicate to varying generations, types of people, and most importantly, to people who had no relationship with God. Nothing seemed more inclusive, cross-generational, simple, timeless, and easy to understand than Oklahoma City Community Church. On top of that we were surprised that name wasn't already taken!

Our ultimate hope as a church is to bring life to our city! We want to be people who don't just say we love our neighbors, but we want to be the best neighbors in the hood. We are exploring what it looks like to see our schools, offices, community/civic groups, coffee shops, and neighborhoods as places brimming with the potential to do things that matter for the kingdom and to bring life to those people and places! We are just getting started, but the stories are starting to pour out, and we are witnessing God rumble across our landscape and begin to disrupt the mundane and mediocre. We are seeing people respond to the silent beckoning that is bidding people to come and pursue the challenging yet fulfilling journey towards life abundantly.

This church is a result of God stirring Christie and I to get off high center and do something with our lives. We initially never wanted to plant a church (it's too much work). The prospect of setting up chairs every week and crossing our fingers that I wasn't going to be giving my weekly message to an empty room with only Christie and my kids sitting on the front row didn't sound too exciting. I can honestly say the dream of planting a church wasn't my dream; however, when you allow questions like "What am I doing" and "Who am I becoming?" to become a real prayer, God will do things you never saw coming.

So this church is what most people would say we *do*. We do other things too, but if someone asked us, "What do you do?"

We would have to say we lead OKC Community Church. I guess that's what we *do*.

꙳꙳꙳

Our journey to doing was preceded by a journey of becoming.

As a pastor, I often have the privilege of having a cup of coffee with others at some trendy, hip coffee shop. Conversations are an important part of the job, and nothing helps a conversation like a nice cup of joe. Inevitably, these conversations are about *life,* but they are rarely about how life is too good, or about how life is just too easy. Instead, these coffee-induced meetings are often shaky conversations about trying to figure out what the future holds. The future is a place full of potential and hope, but it is also a worrisome place for many because it holds the keys to our success and worth.

Nearly every one of these conversations about the future is a quest to figure out *what to do* and how to discover the will of God. At some point (usually after a thoughtful look out the window and a dramatic drink of coffee), I'll simply change the question and ask, "Who are you becoming?"

The question of *who am I becoming* is a life-changing type of question. This question must be *fully* understood in order to *fully* answer it. It isn't asking what you will do with your life. It isn't even simply trying to define the idea of *being* versus *doing*. It's deeper than all of that. It's a question that truly can become a barometer of having a life well-lived. The pursuit of answering this question becomes a primary guide to doing things that matter.

For me this question began in 2003 when a mentor of mine asked me this very question. For whatever reason, it struck me.

Who am I becoming?

When you begin to peel the layers back and allow the question to speak to your life and soul, you begin to ask questions like, "Who am I becoming as a spouse, a friend, a parent, a leader, an employee, and a neighbor?"

I want you to consider your life currently and ask yourself, "Do you like who you are becoming?"

More specifically, do you believe you are becoming who God created you to be?

You may be wondering, "How do I know who God created me to be?"

Most of us struggle to figure this out, but we do know when we aren't who God created us to be. This question isn't designed to create a defeated heart about any failures in your life. Instead, it's intended to give purpose and direction to what lies ahead.

In Philippians, Paul writes a promise that speaks to the plans that lie ahead.

> He who began a good work in you will carry it on to completion until the day of Christ Jesus. (Philippians 1:6 NIV)

God has *created* you for a good work. Many of us suffer with insecurities, broken families, the pain of what's happened in the past, the pain of what is happening right now, the feeling of failure, the feeling of rejection, and in the end we wonder what has happened to who we thought we were going to become.

What ever happened to my dreams?

Yet we read a promise, "He who began a good work in you will carry it on to completion." This promise sounds good, but we don't know what to do with it. It doesn't really answer anything. It just sounds like a promise of something in the future, but what about right now?

God must have a plan, right?

God must be up to something with each of us.

Before I made you in your mother's womb, I chose you.
Before you were born, I set you apart for a special work.
(Jeremiah 1:5, NCV)

That sounds like another great promise, but why doesn't it seem that we are all clued in on this special work? How do we discover God's will or his dream for us? How do we become who we are supposed to become?

Some of you aren't sure that whole "special work" thing even pertains to you.

These are real questions that we face in life. Now granted some life decisions aren't that tough. We aren't praying over whether to eat tacos or burgers for lunch. There are many decisions that are much more difficult than where to eat lunch (although that can be surprisingly difficult at times). We often find ourselves standing at the intersections of our life, wondering, "Will I ever know if I'm doing what God wants me to do?"

We may even be brave enough to back up and ask another question.

Does God even care? Does he even have a plan for our life while we're here on this planet? And if he does have a plan for the seasons of my life, can a regular person like me ever figure it out?

"For I know the plans I have for you," declares the Lord,
"plans to prosper you and not to harm you, plans to give
you hope and a future." (Jeremiah 29:11, NIV)

Now this verse is the king of all feel-good scriptures, but let's get real, it still doesn't clue us in on our special work, or the plans he has for each of us.

I'm learning that maybe discovering God's will and his dream for us is not that complicated as we make it. Maybe we make it way too difficult. Maybe it's not like trying to understand a god-sized Rubik's cube (could never figure those out). Maybe when he said, "I know the plans I have for you," he wasn't talking about somebody else.

ॐ.ॐ.ॐ

Exodus 14

This brings us to the well-known story of the Israelites dramatic escape from Egypt. The story unfolds throughout the initial chapters of Exodus and by the time we get to chapter fourteen, God has done a laundry list of incredible things. He's sent plagues, done miracles, and used Moses in a number of powerful ways. In the midst of God sending plagues and wreaking havoc in Egypt, the pharaoh finally relents and grants permission to Moses for the Israelites to leave. He sets them free.

So the Israelites abandon their slave camps and begin their journey.

Not long into their journey, the Scriptures say that the pharaoh's heart hardens again, and he decides to gather his army and hunt down the Israelites in order to recapture them and bring them back to work on his elaborate Egyptian buildings.

> As Pharaoh approached, the Israelites looked up, and there were the Egyptians, marching after them. They were terrified and cried out to the Lord. They said to Moses, "Was it because there were no graves in Egypt that you brought us to the desert to die? (Exodus 14:10-11, NIV)

Allow me to pause on this sentence. I believe verse eleven may be the first use of sarcasm in recorded history. I love it! Let's continue.

> "What have you done to us by bringing us out of Egypt? Didn't we say to you in Egypt, Leave us alone; let us serve the Egyptians? It would have been better for us to serve the Egyptians than to die in the desert!" Moses answered the people, "Do not be afraid. Stand firm and you will see the deliverance the Lord will bring you today. The Egyptians you see today you will never see again. The Lord will fight for you; you need only to be still. Exodus 14:11-14 (NIV)

Say what? Stand Still?

The Egyptians are coming! They are marching after them! This is absolutely the hardest thing he could have told the Israelites to do.

"Hey, everyone…just stay right where you are and whatever you do…do not panic!"

The Israelites are pinned. They have the Red Sea in front of them and the Egyptian army closing in on them. They had few options. No wonder the Israelites were upset with Moses. He brought them out here to die!

I think we often read the stories about God's people, and we imagine a group of blindly faithful people. We assume they are people who trust God every step of the way. Nope, these people are like the rest of us—struggling to trust God every step of the way. They've seen firsthand what the Egyptian army does to people who defy their authority. They must have believed that life was over. No wonder they wished they were back in Egypt.

I imagine none of us have ever been pinned between an ocean and an army who wants to kill us but for the sake of humoring ourselves, let's imagine that we can relate to this story. This moment for the Israelites can compare to our moments when we are at a complete loss. We don't know what to do when life feels like everything is caving in and you are at the end of your rope. Often when we are in moments of chaos, confusion, or fear, we decide that the best plan is to run looking for cover, looking for someone to help, or for some sense of security.

This sounds like some of our lives.

We say things and pray things like:

- God, where are you taking me?

- God, what am I supposed to do?

- God, is this the job that I am supposed to have?

- God, is the relationship that you want me to be in?

- God, I'm worried about tomorrow.

- God, I'm worried about my family.

- God, I'm worried about my health.

- God, I'm worried about my finances.

- God, I'm worried about my kids.

Many of us often wonder what will come of our life. And as a result we worry. We worry about retirement, health care, paying for education, physical health (yours and loved ones), and money to name a few. In Matthew chapter 6, Jesus tells us to not worry, but instead to seek the kingdom first and all the things we worry about will be taken care of.

That's easier said than done.

God has a plan for us. Great!

He has a special work for you. Great!

How the heck do we figure it out?

I've talked with many friends that felt like they were trying to find the needle of God's will in the haystack of life. We worry not only about all the fears life has to offer, but deep down we wonder if we are getting all from life that we ought to be getting.

As kids, we all have a dream about what we want to be when we grow up. So many of us dreamed of becoming a teacher, police officer, the President, an athlete, or a billionaire.

The question at such an early age is what we want to be when you grow up, and we answer the question with an activity of what we would like to do for a career.

Does what we do equate to who we are?

What if we answered *what we want to be when you grow up* with, "I want to *be* kind, humble, courageous, a leader, a great friend, *a terrific lover…of Jesus.*" (Wink, wink).

Maybe, just maybe, God's will for you is a whole lot more about *who you are than what you do or where you go.* I heard that statement years ago in a sermon, and it has stuck with me ever since. God's will is a whole lot more about who you are as a person than what college you go to, or what job you do, or where you go in your life.

Let's be honest here. When we start thinking about God's will and dreams for our life, immediately our minds start going to, "Is it here, is it there? Is it this, is it that? God, I want a plan. I want a blueprint for my life. God, which road am I supposed to go down?"

Let's imagine you are a college student (some reading are actually college students). Undoubtedly one of the first questions people ask a college student is, "What is your major?" What happens next is universal—the answer breeds some form of judgment. If you answer, "Oh, I'm pre-med," people assume that you must be ambitious. If you answer, "I'm majoring in nuclear engineering," people assume you must be very smart; however, if you answer, "General studies," people immediately think, "Oh, bless your heart."

The question of *what do you do* is a difficult one for me personally. When I tell someone that I'm a pastor, the typical response is usually pretty awkward. People are immediately unsure what to say. I think they are running through their memory bank trying to remember what they've done or said in my presence and hoping they haven't done anything *too bad*. Because of this awkwardness, I'm considering changing my answer when someone asks me what I do. I'm thinking about answering the question by telling them that I'm a *shepherd*. This is not lying. Biblically I am fulfilling the role of shepherd.

Once I share that I am a shepherd, I imagine the conversation going like this:

> THE PERSON: Really, you're a shepherd, like you have sheep?
> ME: Yeah, a whole herd of them.
> THE PERSON: Oh really, where is your herd...or shouldn't it be flock?

41

ME: Yes, of course…flock. They are in Oklahoma City.
THE PERSON: Really, you have sheep in Oklahoma City?
ME: Yep, sure do.
THE PERSON: Well, what do you do with these sheep?
ME: We hang out, I talk to them, and I occasionally have coffee with them.

The startled result may not be much different than telling them I'm a pastor! In all seriousness, for years I've done my best to do whatever I can to ask more questions about who people are instead of focusing on what they do.

I believe God is trying to say to each one of us, "Listen! My will begins with you. My primary role, my major focus right now is not so much where you go or what you do, or where you live, it's about who you are."

You can take out your Bible and start to circle some of the passages that talk about God's will or the phrase *God's will*. And you will find that most of them are not about career choices we make. They're about the person we're supposed to become.

For instance, Romans 12:1–2 says, "Therefore, I urge you, brothers and sisters, in view of God's mercy, to offer your bodies"—to offer yourselves—"as a living sacrifice, holy and pleasing to God—this is your true and proper worship. Do not conform to the pattern of this world, but be transformed by the renewing of your mind. Then you will be able to test and approve what God's will is—his good, pleasing, and perfect will" (NIV).

I think Paul, the writer of Romans, is saying, "If you want to know God's will for your life, just give yourself completely and totally as a living and holy sacrifice that you would no longer conform to the cookie cutter mold of everybody else around you. But instead, renew your mind and transform your way of thinking to God's way of thinking. Then you will realize your potential as a human being and be all that God created you to be. That's God's will for your life."

**Give yourself completely and totally to God. Renew my mind and transform my thinking to God's way of thinking.

If you're doing that, then you can lie down every night, no matter where you are or what you are doing, and know that you're living in the center of the will of God.

It's easy to say this, but I know sometimes this doesn't answer the questions like, "Should I quit my job," "Should I move," "Should I go back to school?"

We want and feel like we need answers right now.

Perhaps discovering God's will and living into the dreams he has for your life begins by saying to God, "Lord, I just want you to make me the person you want me to be. So that whether I do option a, b, or c, I am becoming the person that you want me to be."

Let's go back to Exodus 14.

> Then the Lord said to Moses, "Why are you crying out to me? Tell the Israelites to move. Raise your staff and stretch out your hand over the sea to divide the water so that the Israelites can go through the sea on dry ground. I will harden the hearts of the Egyptians so that they will go in after them. And I will gain glory through Pharaoh and all his army, through his chariots and his horsemen. The Egyptians will know that I am the Lord when I gain glory through Pharaoh, his chariots and his horsemen.
>
> Then the angel of God, who had been traveling in front of Israel's army, withdrew and went behind them. The pillar of cloud also moved from in front and stood behind them, coming between the armies of Egypt and Israel. Throughout the night the cloud brought darkness to the one side and light to the other side; so neither went near the other all night long. (Exodus 14:15-20, NIV)

This incredible miracle raises all sorts of excellent questions. Why doesn't God part the Red Sea when the Egyptian army was still in Egypt?[1] Instead, he waits until the army is in sight.

Why? Why does he wait until the last minute? Seemingly even beyond the last minute? (Does this sound familiar to your life?) Why doesn't God provide the miracle before we know we need it? I think we know the answer to that question. Because we might not recognize His ownership of the miracle.

Why doesn't God give you the answers you need about life when you want them? Why does it feel like everything takes forever to come together? Perhaps because it's in those moments that you realize you have no options but Him. Because He's reminding you that His will for you isn't about giving you answers to the questions you are asking. His will for you is about the person that you are becoming!

Everyone wants a story of God doing something amazing in their lives; however, we don't want to have to walk through the deep struggle of a life that needs a miracle. I'm coming to the conclusion that if my faith journey does not face struggles, I might not be living a life of very much faith.

The Israelites were done. They were in the desert, and it seemed like there is no hope left. They couldn't *do* anything! Life was over unless God's promise was true, and he had actually set them apart for a special work. Sometimes that special work is what He'll do through you, and at other times, that special work is what *He does* and you're just there to be a part of it.

> Then Moses stretched out his hand over the sea, and all that night the Lord drove the sea back with a strong east wind and turned it into dry land. The waters were divided, and the Israelites went through the sea on dry ground, with a wall of water on their right and on their left. (Exodus 14:21–22, NIV)

What? Crazy.

At their most desperate moment, God showed them who he was. God showed them his special work. The special work wasn't their work—it was His work. Not until they had no options and nothing to claim as their own did He truly do the miraculous.

Maybe our dreams shouldn't be filled with what we are going to do. Maybe our dreams should begin with the *special work* that

He is going to do. Maybe we are supposed to think and dream much more about who we are becoming instead of what we are doing.

I've heard so many beautiful dreams. People have shared with me a hope for something better in their community or in this world. People have said that they needed to do something about the plight of a third world nation. I've heard dreams about starting ministries for single moms or for hurting families. People have dreamed with me about starting a small group of their neighbors. People have told me that they felt like God was calling them to leave their jobs and pursue full-time ministry. I've heard dreams about sharing and living their faith out newer, deeper ways. My point is, I've heard a lot of wonderful dreams, and I've had a lot of dream conversations. Unfortunately, they usually end in just that—conversations, words, unrealized special works.

We don't wait for the miracle. We don't dream long enough or pray hard enough to suffer for it. Eventually, most of us turn our attention back to what we know, what we think provides, and what seems logical. Because when we get down the road and it looks like it's going to be tough, we cry, "I wish we were still in Egypt. We'd rather serve the Egyptians than die in the desert!"

This is essentially the way most of us live.

Some of you need to hear that you need to *get out of Egypt*! Your life is not what it should be, could be, and most importantly, you're not becoming who you're supposed to be.

Quit turning around and looking back at Egypt! If what you are doing with your life right now doesn't allow you to be who you ought to be, if you don't like who you're becoming, if the things you do compromise what you hold dearest in life, then you need to get out of Egypt.

Egypt is that place of average faith, which trades in urgent kingdom living for meeting the expectations of others and feeling secure. We must shed the cloak of security.

We need to leave Egypt behind us. It isn't the answer. It isn't better.

I'm not telling you that you have to chase after some dream of doing something crazy in order to do something that matters. I'm actually saying quite the opposite. You need to chase God's will.

> Be joyful always; pray continually; give thanks in all circumstances, for this is God's will for you in Christ Jesus. 1 Thessalonians 5:16 (NIV)

God's will for you is to be joyful, to pray continually, to give thanks. So often we get stuck obsessing over receiving the *guidance* we believe we must have in order to move forward.

"God just give me the answer!" is what we scream. You've been there, right? I believe he's saying back to us, "But I've already spoken so much that you are not acting on."

The answers
to what we are seeking
lie within our being.

I don't know about you, but I have found myself spinning my wheels throwing up a bunch of mud but getting no traction. We must begin acting on what God has already spoken. Not just through His word but also in the simple things He is saying to us. When I've prayed for specific guidance to a question or need, it never fails that I receive guidance about *being*. It's as if He's saying, "I have you. If you will just be who I've created you to be then I will take care of you and reveal the answers you seek. Just *be* and do what I am speaking to you."

While seeking the Lord about something specific such as a decision I need to make, I continually receive guidance about other seemingly unrelated things such as to encourage a friend, serve a certain way, pray with my wife, or be intentionally kind to someone. You know, *things that matter.*

These often become the things the Lord *is* speaking, and if I only seek to hear the answers to my specific questions, I ignore what He *is* saying.

Our answers lie within being.

I'm sure you can relate with wanting to finally peer around the corner and see the big reveal of what's next in your life. We want our dreams to finally become reality! We picture it like having a curtain pulled back and finally seeing what we've been praying and hoping for.

Thankfully, there will be breakthrough moments where we will finally turn the corner and have the exhilaration of some discovery; however, it will not be long before we notice the next corner down the road, and we will seek to journey towards it. I believe for many of you the corner down the road will always be there. It will become your reality.

※ *God having more in store around the corner will be a reality for the entirety of your life.*

This is a great thing! The journey will only keep getting better! Every discovery and step down the journey feeds the desire to keep becoming more of the person God has created you to be.

Pursuing the question of *who am I becoming* simply requires you to consider who God wants you to be within the various roles and circumstances you find yourself in throughout life. My personal journey of pursuing this question led me to dream about who I was becoming as a father, husband, friend, and so on. I remember pulling out my journal and writing down the various titles I carry in life, and I dreamt about who God had created me to be within those contexts.

For example, I asked myself, "Who am I becoming as a leader?" I began writing dreams to that question. Sometimes I wrote my dreams out in bullet points and sometimes paragraphs. The point is that I was dreaming. I began seeing my life with greater depth, purpose, and intentionality.

My dreams were growing. I was dreaming about life instead of success. I was dreaming about life instead of what I *do*. I was dreaming about life instead of reaching for what I didn't know.

I was awakening to the reality that my life as a spouse, parent, friend, leader, neighbor, child, and consumer was like a simmering pot waiting for the heat to be cranked up, so it could boil over. I sensed God wanted to release his power in my life *by being transformed*, much like the release of power when water is boiled and *transformed* into steam.

The world has largely limited the understanding of dreams to being associated with entrepreneurial endeavors or highly creative imagineers (thank you, Disney). Dreaming can't be limited to the creation of products, profits, or a successful life.

> The world is waiting for you
> to unleash your God-given ability
> to *dream* about and for the people
> and places you intersect *every day*.

Imagine who you could become for those people and those places. Who am I becoming is not a question about answering the mysteries of the future, but it's about dreaming and being the person you and I can be *right now*.

Get a journal and dream.

Ask yourself, "Who am I becoming as a…"

- Parent
- Spouse
- Neighbor
- Leader
- Friend
- Teammate
- Sibling
- Customer

- Employee
- Consumer
- American (or whatever country you reside)
- Activist
- Child
- Dreamer
- Believer
- Coach
- Boss
- Servant
- Student

Feel free to add your own titles, roles, or circumstances of life.

These considerations have led me to new discoveries, practices, moments, and stories. I've learned my neighbors' names and thrown block parties because of it. I've intentionally asked more thoughtful questions of others. I've considered my resources and money on a global scale and given more away. I've done things I never thought I'd do. I've prayed for people *in the moment* at coffee shops, in hallways, on the phone, and in the middle of crowds. I've had more meaningful conversations with my children. I've read Scripture looking to learn about who God is and who we are supposed to be. I've embodied kindness more authentically. I've given away my time, wisdom, leadership, encouragement, and work more selflessly. I've texted with the purpose to speak life. I've clung to the simple leadings the Lord gives. I've prayed with my wife more frequently and sincerely. I've celebrated God's goodness more naturally. I've changed my schedule to be a better father. I've found more joy in my everyday responsibilities. I've discovered new purposes in the mundane minutes of my days. I've turned off the television and noise in my life to better hear from the Lord. I've said no to things that rob me of something better. I've said yes to things that were scary but right. I've purposefully rested. I've written this book. I've scheduled my week to have space to intentionally connect and invest in people. Christie and I have started a church with a community of people. I've sought out mentors in my life. I've been a mentor to others. I've fasted. I've stepped away from securities and safety nets. I trusted that God has me.

I've also failed many times. I've been confused, hurt, angry, and restless. I don't tell you the list above to boast about anything because my honest assessment of myself knows I have nothing to boast about except what God has done in my life. My life is still messy, and I can look up and see I still have a long climb ahead of me, but God's promise in Philippians 1:6 is peeking through.

Some of us think that radical faith requires doing something radical.

What if you didn't have to do something like quit your job, move to a third world nation, or give away your inheritance to the poor, in order to be radical? What if you could live in the same place, doing some of the same things, but radically transform it by the person that you are?

Perhaps radical faith is actually doing what God has already said for us do?

The Israelites stood their ground as Moses instructed. If it was up to them, they would have went back to Egypt. But at the last possible moment, God finally did the miraculous. Maybe there are special works all around us. Maybe there are Red Sea's waiting to be split, but God is saying before I can do that special work I desire you to be and do the things, I've already told you to be and do.

Pursue the question of, "Who am I becoming?"

Create space in your life, dream wildly, ask your heavenly Father questions, and listen for His answers. Journal what you hear and read it often. Becoming who God has created you to be is found in the simplicity of being obedient to what he has already spoken. Act on what he is speaking no matter how big or small and become fully you.

❋ Allow God to be God **❋**
and you to be you
because that is exactly who he wants you to be.
Nothing more. Nothing less.

❧·♥·❧

Questions for Reflection And Conversation

1. How would you describe what you do? How would you describe who you want to become?

2. Have you ever struggled while seeking God's will for your life? Describe. How do verses like Romans 12:1–2 and 1 Thessalonians 5:16 shape your understanding of God's will?

3. What are a few things that God has *already spoken* that you need to pursue becoming?

4. Take some time and a journal to dream about who you are *becoming* in throughout the various areas of your life.

CHAPTER THREE

Scale the Walls of Normalcy

S tanding next to a pool table having just finished another
game of nine-ball with a student in my church, I asked what
I thought was a pretty simple question.

"What is your dream?"

I remember him looking at me and then looking down to the
floor. After a long pause, he looked up and said, "I don't know."

He really didn't know. He didn't have any compelling hopes
or dreams. He didn't even have fragments of aspirations that he
could throw out for discussion. He really felt like he had nothing
to say.

This surprised me, and that conversation led me to repeat
the question with other young people. More often than not, I
encountered very vague or even nonexistent aspirations. This
doesn't add up with the stereotype of young people being idealistic dreamers, who are full of hope. We've all witnessed energy
be conjured up among young people for *someone else's* dream, but
what about your dream?

Doing things that matter often begins with a dream—a dream
for something different, new, or better. For me, it began with a
dream to become *who* he wanted me to be. I didn't need to be
them or him. I am the only one who can be me, and that is a
pretty remarkable thing. Likewise, only you can be you because
there's no other you. So pursuing *who* God has created you to be
ends up with a remarkable person. Once we are who we should
be, then what?

I said in the first chapter that every dream begins with some form of discontent, frustration, compassion, hunger, desperation, or pain. Those things are often the spark that God uses to inspire a dream.

Everyone can dream. The ability to dream is an incredibly fascinating gift. Think about it; in your mind, you can quickly transport yourself to a beautiful vacation spot. Go ahead and imagine the vacation of your dreams.

Are you on the beach? Are you in the mountains? Are you at the lake? Are you traveling through Europe? Are you on a wild adventure in Australia, Africa, or deep in the Amazon? Are you at home on your couch?

Go ahead. Picture it. Quit reading and do it.

…

…

…

All right, come back. Pretty slick thing, huh? Without airfare, overpriced luggage fees, or security checks, you were able in just in a few moments to go long distances. You were probably tanned up and a few pounds lighter too! With our power of imagination we can travel the world, build our dream home, hit the game winning shot, or create a business. We've all been given this amazing gift to dream.

On August 28, 1963, one of the greatest dreams of the past few hundred years captured the hearts of millions. Dr. Martin Luther King Jr. shared his dream on the steps of the Lincoln Memorial in Washington D.C. Here's a small portion of that beautiful dream.

> Let us not wallow in the valley of despair, I say to you today, my friends. And so even though we face the difficulties of today and tomorrow, I still have a dream. It is a dream deeply rooted in the American dream.

I have a dream that one day this nation will rise up and live out the true meaning of its creed: "We hold these truths to be self-evident, that all men are created equal."

I have a dream that one day on the red hills of Georgia, the sons of former slaves and the sons of former slave owners will be able to sit down together at the table of brotherhood.

I have a dream that one day even the state of Mississippi, a state sweltering with the heat of injustice, sweltering with the heat of oppression, will be transformed into an oasis of freedom and justice.

I have a dream that my four little children will one day live in a nation where they will not be judged by the color of their skin but by the content of their character.

I have a dream today![1]

I have a dream has become a beacon of hope and change. I often wondered if dreams like King's are reserved for just one or two in every generation. Dreams like his don't come with instruction manuals or any assurances of success. Dreams like these are not accompanied by numbered containers of paint and a canvas with lines and numbers all over it.

As a kid I loved paint-by-numbers projects. In just a short amount of time, I could create a masterpiece. The correct shading, coloring, and proportions were only a few simple steps away. Once I completed my paint-by-numbers canvas, I would proudly display the art as my own; however as we grow older, no one tries to claim a paint-by-numbers piece of art as their own, in fact, no one would even call it art. Once you reach double digits in age, you aren't kidding anyone with your perfectly painted horse majestically standing in front of scenic waterfall. Eventually, we all outgrow paint-by-numbers. True artists are the ones who can take a blank canvas and create something from their imagination. Real art never comes with a step-by-step process.

⁂

I've always marveled at the story of Helen Keller. She was struck deaf and blind by a childhood sickness at only nineteen months old. Living a life unable to see or hear doesn't sound like living to most of us, but to learn her story is an invitation into what humans are truly capable of *seeing*. Her teacher and companion for much of her life was a woman named Anne Sullivan (visually impaired herself), who taught her motions on the palms of her hands to identify objects and words. Amazingly, Keller learned to communicate to the tune of authoring twelve books, being the first deaf and blind person to receive a Bachelor of Arts degree, becoming a lecturer, and a political activist.

One of her most famous quotations is, "The most pathetic person in the world is someone who has sight, but no vision."[2] Her story is nothing less than inspiring about the human capacity to have vision.

Are dreamers like this rare? Are MLK or Keller-type dreams reserved for just a few? Is dreaming wildly something that most of us are relegated to the numbered buckets of paint, or do we have the right and ability to dream wildly? Can anyone be an artist?

I introduced Jeremiah 1:5 in the previous chapter: "Before I made you in your mother's womb, I chose you. Before you were born, I set you apart for a special work" (NCV).

We all want to discover our special work, but do we all have one? Ever since the pool table discussion, I've been burdened. *I believe many of us claim dreams, but few chase dreams.* In the end, I rarely hear an original thought, I rarely hear a passionate plea for change, I rarely hear pure excitement about new ground covered, and I rarely see or hear about anything that shakes the world around us. I believe there are times we must all ask ourselves, "What am I dreaming about?" "Have I obliviously claimed a paint-by-numbers project as my own masterpiece?"

Call me a bit of a conspiracy theorist, but I believe the world is dictating and tailoring our dreams more than we realize. We've been duped by what I call the *conspiracy of normalcy*. Simply stated, we are expected to be normal. The world places numerous expectations of normalcy on us. Our schools, parents, family, friends, and society has placed a host of good and some not-so-good expectations on us. We are expected to do life a certain way, make certain grades, earn a certain amount of money, have a certain level of home, and the list goes on and on.

There are many *American Dream* messages given to young people about becoming whatever they want to be, but in the end, it seems like most trade in wild dreams for the standards of American living that is typically more about keeping up with Jones's and less about dreaming.

We all want a measure of normal, but do we want our whole life to be normal?

I don't think so.

I think we all desire the exhilarating experience of creating a masterpiece with God. We wonder, "What's my unique dream, or how am I going to leave my fingerprint on this world?"

Am I suggesting we can all become like Martin Luther King Jr.?

Of course not, but I know that God has created us for more than what most of us are living. Too many of us have been sucked into a normal life. As a result, we find ourselves chasing the American standard of normal instead of reimagining what's possible.

Be wary of becoming a *casualty* of normalcy.

The conspiracy of normalcy begins early in life. It begins creeping in on our children before we even realize it; however, we weren't created to live this way. When we were children, we had an amazing ability to dream. I'm sure when you were a child you dreamed and imagined all the time. You probably had imaginary friends or dreamed that you were a doctor, a ballerina, a celebrity, a cowboy, a princess, or an athlete.

As a boy, I can remember imagining I was standing at home plate with a bat in my hand. It was the World Series, and it was the bottom of the ninth, two strikes, two outs, bases loaded, and down by three runs. In my imagination I always hit the game-winning grand slam.

As I'm writing this, I'm thankful that my kids dream (and that the world hasn't beaten it out of them yet). It is incredible to watch them dream and imagine things like parties with all sorts of people (who have all sorts of weird names). Sometimes they have dogs and cats and other times they *are* dogs and cats. When Emily was younger, she even imagined she had a husband. He would go places with us, but he wouldn't ride with us in our car; instead, he would follow us with his truck. Coincidentally, his name was Tim too. The fact that her husband and I had the same name (not to mention the same truck) might be an indicator that her dreams could have used a little creativity, but she was dreaming! As I watch my kids, I am convinced I'm seeing the heart of God for us.

I believe our children provide a glimpse of truth that helps us understand how God created us. Kids are wildly imaginative people who are full of dreams. I believe that as we grow older, our ability to dream is obviously supposed to mature, but I do not believe it is supposed to be suppressed and replaced by more realistic and normal expectations.

In Acts 3, we encounter a story of a crippled man who sits at the entrance gate to the temple. In this particular story, Peter and John are going to the temple to pray and encounter this man.

> One day Peter and Jon were going up to the temple at the time of prayer – at three in the afternoon. Now a man crippled from birth was being carried to the temple gate called Beautiful, where he was put everyday to beg from those going into the temple courts. When he saw Peter and John about to enter, he asked them for money. Peter looked straight at him, as did John. Then Peter said, "Look at us!" So the man gave them his attention, expecting to get something from them. (Acts 3:1–5, NIV)

This was certainly a sly place for a needy person to post up asking for help. He sat at the temple gate hoping those going to pray would feel the extra urge to be generous. I'm sure most days he received enough food or extra coins to survive, but it was just that—survival.

On this particular day, Peter and John walked by him with something he could have never anticipated. Peter looks at him and says, "Look at us!"

He immediately looked up, hoping to receive some money from them. He was looking for what he had always looked for.

Nothing more.

It wasn't enough for Peter and John to drop him a coin. They served a God that was bigger than just survival. This beggar might have only hoped for more of the same old thing, but Peter and John had been with Jesus, and they had experienced more.

> Then Peter said, "silver and gold I do not I have, but what I do have I give to you." (Acts 3:6, NIV)

Don't you know the beggar was like, "If you don't have any silver or gold you better at least have a sandwich!

> "In the name of Jesus Christ of Nazareth, walk." Taking him by the right hand, he helped him up, and instantly the man's feet and ankles became strong. He jumped to his feet and began to walk. Then he went with them into the temple courts, walking and jumping, and praising God. When all the people saw him walking and jumping, and praising God, they recognized him as the same man who used to sit begging at the temple gate called Beautiful, and they were filled with wonder and amazement at what had happened to him. (Acts 3:6b-10, NIV)

He sat at the gate simply wanting money, and Peter and John entered the scene and radically reframed what he should want. They proclaimed that his *mediocre* requests were not good enough, and they showed him the true possibility and power of God.

Peter demanded that the beggar look him in the face, and then Peter proclaims that their God can make the seemingly impossible, possible! The beggar expected nothing more than normal. At times, God will surprise us and catapult us out of normal in spite of our lack of belief or absence of dreams.

Peter and John expected the impossible. The beggar was only a recipient of Peter and John's belief that God could do anything. He happened to be in the path of two dreamers on the way to pray at the temple. Talk about riding someone else's coattails. He didn't do anything abnormal. He was just radically blessed—or lucky. I've often heard people say they don't believe in luck. Well, I think luck exists. I'm pretty sure I've had the experience of dumb luck much like this beggar.

❧·✿·☙

Christie and I were generously given a gift of air travel and show tickets to see Celine Dion in Las Vegas. Celine is one of Christie's favorite artists, so we gratefully accepted the gift.

Now Vegas isn't exactly our scene. I don't say that in a holier-than-thou attitude against Sin City (*great* nickname), but I really don't have a clue about cards or any type of gambling. Prior to our trip to Vegas, my only experience with a casino was on cruise ship when, for the pure novelty of it, we put twenty bucks into a slot machine and won $180 (not too shabby)!

On our last night in Vegas, we decided to put a few bucks in a slot machine again for the pure novelty.

(Are you judging me?)

Before actually playing, we wandered around the casino clueless of where to go or what to do. This was our first and only time in a real casino. We quickly realized there are dozens of types of slot machines. Penny slots, nickel slots, quarter slots, dollar slots, five-dollar slots, and all the way up to high-limit slots where one pull was worth a thousand dollars.

Needless to stay, the high limit slots weren't our destination.

We finally settled in on a quarter slot machine. Christie and I sat down, and we were reluctant to be too aggressive, so I pulled out a five-dollar bill, put it into the machine, and nervously began pushing the button. After two or three minutes of playing and having already lost about two dollars and seventy-five cents, I hit the button and the machine stopped. It literally stopped. Initially I had no clue why it stopped. It's not like the pictures were all cherries or all sevens. I hit the button again and still nothing. I looked at Christie, and she had a concerned look on her face like I had done something to break the machine.

Over our shoulder a stranger shouted, "Are you kidding me? I just got up from that machine!" Then he began muttering a string of words together that even Sin City herself may have been a little embarrassed by.

At that point I realized that something good might have just happened. An older gentleman sitting next to us said, "Just wait here. Don't get up. They will come to you."

Who will come to me? The casino boss and his boys?

At this point, Christie and I are sweating from the uncertainty of the moment. Finally after the longest fifteen minutes of our life, a casino attendant finally walked to our machine. She had zero emotion or energy, and it felt like everything was moving in slow motion.

She finally said, "Congratulations"—a pause. She pushed a key into machine and then another pause—"you won twenty-five hundred dollars."

I should have jumped up and screamed at the top of my lungs, but instead I sat there all cool like I had done this before. Christie and I looked at each other in disbelief. We had won twenty-five hundred dollars on a free trip to Vegas on our first five bucks! We had won the second highest payout the machine could actually do. The attendant counted out twenty-five one-hundred-dollar bills into my hand. I immediately put the money in my pocket.

What happened in Vegas did not stay in Vegas. We gladly took our winnings home.

Just in case you are doing the math, on my only two casino encounters, I invested $25 and received $2680 in return.

For the record, I do not recommend gambling (unless you are with me). Sometimes we are just plain lucky in life. Sometimes timid couples happen to sit down at the right place at the right time. So, let's not confuse luck with dreams.

The story of the beggar at the temple gate called Beautiful is more about Peter and John and their faith that God could use him to do the miraculous. They were dreamers! But what about this beggar, what can we learn from him? He got lucky, I guess, I should say *blessed*. Gratefully, God will do that for us well beyond what we deserve; however, the beggar asked for nothing more than normal.

But what if you asked for more than normal?

You must stop hoping God *blesses* your normal, mediocre expectations about life; instead, dream wildly about doing something with your life that is beyond normal. Swing for the fences. Believe that God has created you for a special work. God makes the impossible, possible! He can do more in one minute of your life than you can do on your own during your entire life.

Enter the story of another beggar.

Bartimaeus was a blind beggar from the city of Jericho. His daily life was very similar to our friend who sat at the entrance of the temple gates. He too sat along the city streets begging and hoping to receive enough to get through another day. Imagine being an outcast your entire life. Society had assumed your family or you had sinned in such a significant way that you were blind as a result. It's suffering on top of suffering.

The story of Bartimaeus is found in Mark 10 on a day that Jesus and his disciples were traveling through Jericho. Imagine the day. The town began to stir as the sun rose and like most mornings, Bartimaeus was awakened by the sounds of the city.

Bartimaeus grabbed his coat and headed towards his regular spot to beg. He had found an area where the people knew him and tolerated his presence. Upon arriving at his spot, he began to do his normal chatting about his unfortunate story to the passers by, pleading for some help. As the day grew later, Bartimaeus became aware of some abnormal commotion and an unusual amount of people crowding into the streets. He listened to the crowd walking by and learned that Jesus of Nazareth was headed his way through the city.

I'm sure he couldn't believe that Jesus was there. He had heard about Jesus, and his first thought turned toward the stories that had spread about the healings Jesus had done throughout the land. I'm sure he wondered if this was his chance to change his life. He listened intently to the crowd so he would know when Jesus was actually near him. He braced himself as Jesus approached.

> When he heard that it was Jesus of Nazareth, he began to shout, "Jesus Son of David, have mercy on me!" Many rebuked him and told him to be quiet, but he shouted all the more, "Son of David, have mercy on me! (Mark 10:47–48, NIV)

The crowd normally tolerated Bartimaeus, but this was not the time.

"Don't bother Jesus! Shut your mouth, Bartimaeus!"

How often have our dreams been thwarted by the people around us? Haven't we been told to think more realistically or to stick to what we know? We've been told to shut up on more than one occasion. Often the people around us unknowingly anchor us to normal because they avoid the abnormal in their own lives. If the people around you are voices that *box you into normal* in the name of love then you should consider that their love may have the wrong intentions. They may not be thinking about you as much as they are worrying about themselves and their addiction to keeping the status quo.

Jesus stopped and said, "Call him." So they called to the
blind man, "Cheer up! On your feet! He's calling you."
Throwing his cloak aside, he jumped to his feet and came
to Jesus. (Mark 10: 49–50, NIV)

Funny how quick the crowd can turn on your dreams. One
moment they hope to drown it out and crush it, and the next they
cheer you. The crowds cannot be the barometer for the validity or
fervor of the dreams we chase. People will doubt you and at other
times they will cheer you; both can be equally dangerous.

Bartimaeus couldn't believe it. He had actually been acknowledged and called by Jesus. The rumors about Jesus were bigger
than just the miracles: the stories claimed he was the Messiah!
Bartimaeus approached Jesus nervously. He stood in front of
Jesus and was immediately asked, "What do you want me to do
for you?" (Mark 10:51)

This was the biggest question of his life.

It seemed obvious to us what he would want, but remember
Bartimaeus has been asking for things his entire life. Every day
he begged for money, food, clothing, shelter and anything else
to help him survive. Would Bartimaeus see this as a different
moment, or would he ask for nothing more than normal?

He answered the question, "Rabbi, I want to see."

Bartimaeus understood who he was talking to. He was talking to the King of kings, and he was requesting Him to enable
the biggest dream of his life. In this moment Jesus changed what
Bartimaeus cared about. He didn't care about normal. He opened
the possibilities to beyond normal. Jesus made the seemingly
impossible possible. This was no ordinary moment, and it called
for a dream that was about more than survival, and Bartimaeus
seized the moment. I believe it is no coincidence that his dream
was about vision.

What I like about Bartimaeus's miracle is that it wasn't about
luck. He asked for beyond normal. He dreamed wildly.

Jesus is asking us, "What do you want me to do for you?" and I believe many of us are answering requests for him to provide money or to give us a little happiness or a better job, and essentially all we are asking for is more of what we already have— more normal.

Really? Is that enough? Are we approaching Jesus like he is the King of kings, or are we acting like he is anyone else who walks by us? We must believe for him to do immeasurably more than we would ask of anyone else or even of ourselves.

> God can do anything, you know—far more than you could ever imagine or guess or request in your wildest dreams! He does it not by pushing us around but by working within us his Spirit deeply and gently within us. (Ephesians 3:20, The Message)

The greatest moments of our lives must not be dictated by mere luck or by riding the coattails of other peoples' dreams who we happen to intersect, but rather we must seize the invitation of our heavenly Father to dream wildly and trust that He is waiting to create a masterpiece with us.

Remember the words from Jeremiah, "Before I made you in your mother's womb, I chose you. Before you were born, I set you apart for a special work." (Jeremiah 1:5)

We must take on the heart of Bartimaeus to believe in a God that can do anything. God is inviting you to see your life in a way that paints beyond the lines and ignores the numbers.

Your life was designed as a blank canvas. God created each of us with unlimited possibility. As children, we learn how to dream, and God began to work within us, readying us for the special work of our lives. As we grew older, our dreams were often squelched, and we were told to "grow up." The people around us told us to consider more sensible and responsible careers and to place any audacious dreams on the backburner. We make excuses for letting dreams go and accepting a normal life by blaming our surroundings, background, or family. In the end, most of us choose to turn in our blank canvas for an alternative canvas with black lines and little numbers all over it. We've decided this makes life easier. We are allowed to simply follow the prescribed action steps, and it will result in a life that has the correct shading, coloring, and proportions. Once completed we act like we've created it, but we end up leading an unsatisfied life knowing the truth of what we've painted with our lives. The journey of joining God in the creation of a masterpiece seems too daunting for most, so we settle for normalcy.

We are, therefore, sadly left with a world full of canvases that was supposed to resemble the majesty of the world-famous Louvre museum. Instead, we are left with very average, nontransformative, and hardly impressive collection of knock-off paintings. The world is more reflective of the mass-produced art section at Wal-Mart, which clearly leaves the world shrugging and looking around for something more.

> The world is in need of Christ followers
> who will leave behind
> mediocre versions of living,
> and relentlessly scale the walls of *normalcy*
> for the purposes of God's Kingdom.

What if you recaptured your God-given ability to dream? Who and what would you imagine becoming? The blank canvas sits quietly waiting for you to unroll it and begin dreaming with your Creator.

Jesus is waiting for you to call out to him so He can reply, "What do you want me to do for you?"

I'm not suggesting He's eagerly waiting to grant you three wishes like He's some genie in a bottle. Instead, I am fanning the flame in your heart to hear from God about the dreams He wants to ignite in your life.

You only have one life to live, and no one is responsible for it but you. The possibilities that God has with your life are only limited by the parameters you place around it. What if you allowed the seemingly impossible to become possible? Dreaming wildly for the purposes of something bigger and more meaningful than the American Dream is where God-sized dreams are born. What if you dreamed about the seemingly impossible to become possible within your faith, family, career, relationships, and future?

✳✳ Your dreams matter. Your dreams will lead you to do things that matter. Your dreams will lead you to a life that matters. Becoming who God has created you to be is a pursuit of the ever-evolving dreams that God places within your soul. Dreams are not a one-time discovery, but they become the unfolding story of your life. Pursue your masterpiece one brush stroke at a time with your heavenly Father. ✳✳

✳ *You only have one life to live* ✳

꙳⋆꙳

Questions for Reflection And Conversation

1. How has the idea of normalcy impacted decisions you've made about your faith, family, career, relationships, or future?

2. How do your prayers and requests to God resemble the blind beggar at the temple gate? Are they too small? Too normal?

3. If you considered Jesus asking you, "What do you want me to do for you?" what/how would you respond?

4. Have you followed the prescribed action plan provided by others for your life more than you've considered the blank canvas that God has given you to create a masterpiece with him? If so, describe.

THE SECOND PART

LIVE DIFFERENTLY

*What if everyday you made choices
that caused you to live differently?*

CHAPTER FOUR

Living the Gospel

When I was a kid, my friends and I often went to the community pool to cool off during hot summer days. At the deep end of the pool, three diving boards stood ominously challenging every little kid that dared climb their steps. In the middle of these three boards stood the high dive, sixteen terror-filled feet above the water. I can still remember the fear of climbing that high dive for the first time, uncertain if I would actually survive the ordeal.

As I inched out towards the edge all sorts of alarms were blaring within me saying, "Stop you idiot!"

This particular diving board wasn't a solid platform. No, it was a springboard that made each step towards the edge a wobbly nightmare. The edge is a dangerous, scary place. It's much easier to simply dip our toe into the pool than to look down the barrel of the high dive, but for my friends and I, it was a right of passage—one where not jumping was more detrimental than jumping. It was a bad day for the poor kid that chose to turn around and climb back down the ladder and shamefully slip back into the shallow end of the pool.

It's strange how many times I've stood at the edge of something in life such as the edge of a decision, a moment of trust, uncertainty about the future, and even the edge of my own faith. Similar to the feelings I had on that high dive, fear, concern, and impending danger are all in front of me, but nonetheless I have the conviction to jump.

Before we jump, let's pause.

Let's pause to consider why and where the conviction to make these jumps in life come from. I can't help but state the obvious—becoming a person who does something that matters every day requires a life that is *different*. It will require moments that your faith leads you to do things you thought you could never do. Moments of unbridled trust, obedient action, overwhelming love, and at times, moments where we have to jump!

The four values in this book—*dream wildly, live differently, love recklessly, and lead courageously*—all sit under the umbrella of *Doing Things That Matter*, however, I'd be selling the story short if I didn't share how these values came to be. Live Differently was actually the original statement that started it all for me. Before there was any dreaming, loving, leading, or doing things that matter, God painted a vision in me that we are to be people who live differently. I often imagined what if everyday we had thoughts, prayed prayers, or made choices that caused us to live differently. In the years that followed, the other values naturally linked arms one at a time with this vision to be people who would live differently than the world around us.

The Scriptures are chalked full of stories that point us to become people who live differently. They also show us that we have a God who acts differently. He does justice differently. He does love differently. He does acceptance, forgiveness, purpose, hope, and even religion differently. Perhaps that's why Jesus was constantly ripping at the foundations that the Pharisees and religious leaders were building. Maybe, Jesus came to establish something different.

So is different good?

Now, there are some things in life that are classified as different that are actually just plain weird. For instance, pro wrestling is not necessarily a good different. It's a weird different. The taste of tofu is not a good different. It's a weird different. But in the case of the gospel, the different is the difference between good and bad, hopeful and hopeless, forgiveness and bitterness, and love and hate.

At times being different will seem crazy. It will seem over the top, extreme, and at times, it may seem strange. Maybe that's why Peter said we would be like *aliens and strangers in this world*. People may not understand some of the things faithful followers of Jesus do, say, and believe, but the hope is that *our different becomes a good different*. Things like loving our neighbor, forgiveness, and caring for the broken become very good things that are actually countercultural from the world we live in.

In Genesis chapter 22 we find a story about Abraham and his son Isaac. Abraham was the sole human being on the planet who had access and relationship with the Creator God. God promised Abraham to make him the father of a great nation. God would be their God, and they would be his people. Prior to Genesis 22, Abraham and his wife, Sarah were unable to have a child and were ready to throw in the towel and give up. Little did they know about the miracle God had in store for them. At the ripe age of one hundred, Abraham and Sarah experienced the miracle of God's promise and had a son. They named him Isaac. I imagine this kid was spoiled! Isaac was a gift. He was Abraham's legacy.

I may have a slight ability to relate to the emotions that Abraham must have felt. Our first three children were all girls. Nothing makes you feel like more of a superhero than having three girls. I was completely happy being a father to princesses, but the one lingering thought about not having a son was that the Mannin name was hanging in the balance of my offspring. I happened to be the last Mannin in our family tree. Unless there is some rogue tree branch of Mannin's out there that we don't know about, I stood as the last Mannin with the potential to keep this tree from dying. Assuming our daughters would take the name of their future husbands, it looked like this tree may be coming to a withery end. So when Greyson came along as child number four,

I appropriately nicknamed him, *The Legacy,* to honor his role of keeping the family name officially moving on.

Isaac was the legacy.

But then God threw a nasty curveball that Abraham could have never saw coming.

> Some time later God tested Abraham. He said to him, "Abraham! "Here I am," he replied. Then God said, "Take your son, your only son, whom you love—Isaac—and go to the region of Moriah. Sacrifice him there as a burnt offering on the mountains I will show you. (Genesis 22:1–2, NIV)

Imagine being Abraham in this moment. This would be a terribly horrifying and confusing moment. Why would God ask such a thing? The relationship between God and Abraham was certainly different. During this ancient time, the people of the world had no idea who the Creator God was. God had interacted with very few people (that we know of).

Abraham's culture understood little gods. People worshipped all sorts of gods—the god of the sea, the god of the sky, and the god of cats, or was it that the cats were the gods? Anyway, you get it. There were many gods.

This was Abraham's world. Yet, here he is communicating with something that seems different than these other gods. This God claimed to be the one true God and the Creator of the universe. Abraham has seemingly found favor with God, but now God has asked him to do the unthinkable!

Abraham is standing at the edge of a jump. God has thrown down the gauntlet. Sacrifice your son.

Abraham becomes a hero of faith in this moment. Abraham saddled up his donkey, packed enough wood for the burnt offering he would have to perform, and took his only beloved son Isaac and headed towards the mountains of Moriah.

Upon arriving near the base of the mountain, Abraham unloaded the donkey and Isaac carried the wood and the knife up the mountain. Once they reached the top, Abraham built an altar, and I imagine Isaac helped—*Isaac helped.* Isaac is not a child in this story. Most sources point to Isaac not being the small child we sometimes picture, but more than likely close to twenty years old.[1] A small boy could not carry enough wood on his back up a mountain to make an altar. At some point while putting the altar together, Isaac figured it out. He must have.

> It says that Abraham *"bound his son Isaac and laid him on the altar.* (Genesis 22:9)

Trust me. there is no way that a man who is well over one hundred years old is subduing an unwilling young man and binding him on an altar. Isaac willingly does it.

Who is the hero? Or should it be *heroes?*

We must remember that Abraham was in an ancient world. There were no scriptures at this point. No law from the Lord had been provided. This story about child sacrifice seems odd and out of the character of God. It's easy to wonder why is it even in the Bible. We must remember Abraham's world. He is used to seeing a culture that worshiped all sorts of gods and often within this ancient culture child sacrifice was not all that uncommon.

We find examples of this barbaric practice existing in other places throughout the Old Testament (see 2 Kings 3:27, 21:6, 23:10).

Several forms of idol worship included offering children to the gods—mostly to appease their anger against humanity.

The history of the Israelites proves that the sacrifice of children would be a horrific act. In Leviticus 20:2–5, we find harsh instructions and Israeli law against child sacrifice. God's nature was not inclined to receive human sacrifices offered to Him; however Abraham died about 245 years before Moses ever showed up on the scene. So Abraham had never read Leviticus or any law from God. Abraham has only had the example of how others worshipped their gods.

So it's possible when Abraham was called by God to sacrifice his son that he wasn't too surprised. I'm sure he wasn't excited about the prospect or eager to sharpen the knife, but he was aware that many people had sacrificed children in the name of their god. So now, perhaps, his God was asking him to do the same.

For Christie and I our kids are the most precious things we have in this world. The thought of anything happening to any one of my kids is the scariest and darkest possibility that exists. It's impossible to imagine not having one of them in our lives. If you have children, you can relate to this feeling. I have some friends who had to walk through the difficult struggle of losing their precious daughter to cancer. As friends we hurt for them. We grieved for them; however we knew we couldn't feel what they felt. I can't imagine many things on this earth more painful or hellish than losing a child. Abraham is on top of the mountain, with his son bound to an altar, and he is holding the knife. Why is God doing this? What is he up to?

Amazingly, Abraham and Isaac go all the way. In verse ten it says that Abraham, *"reached out his hand and took the knife to slay his son..."*

At that point a voice calls out from heaven:

"Abraham! Abraham!"

"Here I am," he replied.

"Do not lay a hand on the boy," he said.

"Do not do anything to him. Now I know that you fear God, because you have not withheld your son, your only son."

This is one of those intense stories that preaches! It has tension, drama, truth, faith, and in the end, everyone wins. Not only is Abraham the hero, but so is Isaac, and due to his last second save, so is God. Like I said, everyone wins. This is how we like it to go, don't we? Even if we endure hardship and are tested in life, we expect things to turn up like we want, *winning,* standing on top of the summit of Mt. Everest saying it was worth the effort and sacrifice.

Can I remind you that not all have survived the climb?

Sometimes we never are willing to saddle up the donkey or pick up the knife. And let's be honest, sometimes if we do saddle up the donkey, take the journey, and pick up the knife, we don't like the outcome.

What happens when things don't turn out like we want them to?

What happens when we don't all win?

What happens when the jump off the high dive is into an unexpectedly empty pool?

Maybe the answers to those questions are found by asking a different question.

Why?

Why did God have Abraham do this?

If God never wanted a child sacrifice and if he was going to stop Abraham at the last moment anyway, why does he have Abraham and Isaac go through this whole ordeal? The obvious answer that we've all heard is that he was testing Abraham's faith. There's certainly truth in that. It's easy to see that God was testing Abraham's willingness to obey at any cost? We get that.

Maybe God was also showing Abraham something else. Perhaps, He was showing Abraham that this God is different than other gods. Maybe one of the messages here is that this God isn't angry. He isn't like the other idols of worship in Abraham's ancient world. This God will do things differently than what people expect.

God was establishing with Abraham a new way to be human. God was establishing with Abraham a new way to see God.

It's as if God said to Abraham and to the generations to come, "I am not going to make you sacrifice your son. I am not here to take from you. In fact, it is not you who will suffer. I will be the one to suffer and sacrifice my son. I'm here to give to you."

Centuries later, a different son carried wood on his back for his own sacrifice. He walked through Jerusalem, which happened to be the ancient region of Moriah, and he walked up a hill called Golgotha. He was mercilessly whipped and beaten, and he willingly walked to his own death.

He had a Father who could have stopped it.

He, himself could have even stopped it.

But Jesus knowingly allowed himself to be bound by ropes and placed upon an altar. The altar of sacrifice was in the form of a cross. The brutality of his sacrifice dwarfs the proposed sacrifice of Isaac. Jesus was violently nailed to the cross by nine-inch square iron spikes.

At no point, did a voice call out from heaven.

Not while he was being beaten. Not during his outrageous trial. Not while he was whipped, spit on by his own creation, or while he struggled to carry his cross through the city and up the hill. Not even when the Roman guards *lifted their hands* armed with hammers and spikes.

No voice came then either.

We have a God who is different than anything else the world knows. We serve a God that continues to say I am not like the other gods of this world. Maybe in some metaphorical or symbolic way, each of us are represented by Isaac in this story. Like Isaac, we are the ones who deserve death, but God has spared us and He provided another way. That's the easy way to understand how we relate to Isaac, but is there more?

Well, as I stated earlier I believe Isaac helped. At some point on that mountain with Abraham, he figured out what the heck was going down! He allowed his father to bind him and he was *laid down on the altar as a living sacrifice*. So much attention was given to Abraham. We honor him and celebrate his faith.

What about Isaac? After all, it's Isaac who carried the wood on his own back.

> Whoever wants to be my disciple must deny themselves and take up their cross daily and follow me. (Luke 9:23, NIV)

This is one of those a feel-good verses that's on a wooden plaque hanging somewhere in our home. Most of us are familiar with the words of it, but when we consider its implications it should have a tremendous ripple effect. In fact these ripples should be more like tidal waves.

Take up your cross daily or in other words, you should carry the wood on your own back every day. And carrying the cross doesn't mean to make sure you have a cross necklace on to symbolize your faith. When you carry a cross you are actually living a life of sacrifice and surrender. It brings the words of Romans 12:1 to greater life, "Therefore, brothers and sisters, in view of God's mercy, offer yourselves – your bodies as living sacrifices."

Similar to Isaacs walk to the altar and Jesus' walk to Golgotha we must learn to walk sacrificially day in and day out. We often think our faith in Jesus will require sacrifice in the version of giving up the "ways of the world" such as, certain behaviors, activities, or dreams about success, fame, and fortune.

We've trivialized sacrifice
into giving up excess and privilege.

I've heard many people say something like, "I've sacrificed and worked hard to get where I am today."

My question is what did you sacrifice?

I think we know what they mean. They mean they sacrificed a more easygoing lifestyle, maybe they sacrificed watching more television, eating cookies, or they gave up a weekend with friends. In America that's what many believe sacrifice is while we go on with 50inch flat screens, full refrigerators, and overflowing closets. It doesn't sound like brutal sacrifice when we say it that way, does it? At some point our submission to God should come at a cost to our privilege, conveniences, and riches.

> Then he said to them all: "Whoever wants to be my disciple must deny themselves and take up their cross daily and follow me. For whoever wants to save their life will lose it,

but whoever loses their life for me will save it. What good is it for someone to gain the whole world, and yet lose or forfeit their very self? (Luke 9:23–25, NIV).

In order to truly live this passage we may not get to keep everything we want.

We may have to let go of something in order to pick up the cross.

Did you catch that? You may have to let go of something.

It could be the approval of parents or peers. It could be the job that you thought would give you everything you ever wanted. It could be letting go of the pursuit of the American Dream. It could be laying down control. It could be giving up addictions. It could be bitterness. It could be giving away your money.

When you pick up the cross you carry the gospel.

The gospel of Jesus loves our neighbors, helps the poor, cares for the broken, proclaims peace, fights for slaves, captives, and those bound by injustices, heals the sick, gives grace to those who need it, preaches the good news, shines light into the darkness, makes disciples, and restores good.

This is what it means to live the gospel.

The gospel is a beautiful thing. Becoming a person who actually does things that matter for the gospel everyday would shatter the mold of what normal people do. You'd not only live differently, you'd shine for the world to see. What if we truly lived Luke 9:23–25 like it meant something to us?

Being different isn't about being unique or quirky. Rather, it's about being purposed and empowered by the Holy Spirit to be a faithful follower of Jesus who intentionally goes into your world every day as a living and breathing embodiment of the gospel.

The altar where we make our sacrifices to the Lord is obviously and thankfully much different than Abraham and Isaac's altar, but the requirements of our faith are often very similar. God proved to Abraham that he was not like the other gods, but that he was a different kind of God. In turn, he asked Abraham to be different, to submit to *one God* in a culture where it was normal to worship many gods.

Becoming different in a world of vast similarity requires breaking free of the things that hold you down and keep you grounded in the sea of sameness. Think about your life, and I'm certain you can identify things you haven't surrendered but need to. You must posses the courage to let go of the things that anchor you to the safe and familiar. It's time to let go of things that limit your faith. Go ahead and consider areas in your life that need change. Areas that you need to let go of by moving on, getting rid of, forgiving, or forgetting.

What is that that thing, relationship, time consumer, or bitterness that you need to let go of?

Perhaps you have a desire to have a certain societal status or reputation. Maybe you work too much. Maybe things like materialism, greed, jealously, or anger seem to get in the way of the cross.

What do you need to let go of in order to pick up the cross?

Many times we think we are living for Jesus, but all we are doing is carrying around the same things in this life that everyone else is carrying. So even though we love Jesus, we may not be that different, much less a person who is living the gospel or doing things that matter.

Remember the high dive?

It scares us and invites us all at the same time.

It's not easy to jump, because jumping requires us to let go.

Too many people who claim to love Jesus are just dipping their toe into to the pool and claiming that they are swimming. The most dangerous part of the edge of a jump, whether it's a diving board or the edge of a faithful decision is not the jump itself. Rather the most dangerous part of the edge of a jump is the possible retreat. Now there are some moments when a retreat is necessary. There are times when jumping isn't the will of God. But for the moments and decisions that you know God is telling you to go or those moments that you have to get out of the situation you are in—then it's time to jump. When we retreat, we essentially shrink, and we choose to settle for status quo. The decision to retreat is a decision to stop trusting God.

It's time to let go.

Make a change to your life. Be different. Let. It. Go. So you can live the gospel. No retreats.

It's time to jump.

Living differently
is a cannonball into a pool
of uncertainties, questions, and endless possibilities
that a life with Christ has to offer.

≳.✿.≲

Questions for Reflection And Conversation

1. Does being different ever scare or intimidate you? Would you rather blend in? How can being different for Christ not be a weird, strange or bad different?

2. What do you need to let go of in order to pick up the cross?

3. What does it mean for your everyday life to live the gospel?

4. What is that thing in your life that feels like you are at the edge and you need to jump? How will this cause you to live differently? How will this step help you live the gospel?

CHAPTER FIVE

The Church Doesn't Matter

When we first started dreaming about the prospect of planting a church and were imagining what OKC Community Church would become, I kept coming back to this simple hope that we would be a community of people who desire *to be the church the best way we know how*. I realize that this statement might lack a little zeal, pizzazz, or the right kind of spunk to get highly motivated church planting organizations looking for new churches to *launch large* or seek out *big easy wins* (common language in the church planting world); however, there's something about having a hope for the church that's humble, simple, and about giving our best that feels right where we need to be. Shouldn't this be the case for those leading the church no matter if we launch large or launch small?

Paul describes the church as a *she* in Ephesians 5 when he compares a bride and a groom to that of the church (the bride) and Jesus Christ (the groom). The church is an interesting girl. Over the years we've all had questions about her, such as why are there so many different types of churches? Why does she so easily hurt us? Why does she so easily frustrate us? How important is the church to God? Do you have to actually go to church to be a good Christian? Can't you just love God? Why do some churches believe *this* about God while others believe *that*?

Everyone knows that the state of the church in the US is becoming increasingly marginalized, dangerously irrelevant, and even disrespected within culture. For those of us in the church it's hard to always know how to respond to this. Do we fight against the culture that is pushing the church's relevance into oblivion? Do we look ourselves in the mirror and ask what are we doing wrong?

As a believer, I'm tired of the church being known for the flaws of people rather than our truth of the gospel. I'm worn-out witnessing the church being more about a celebrity pastor than the deep work of God's Spirit among a community. The frustration is deep, wide, high, and far — not with the church, but with those within churches that keep fueling the world to ignore what the church has to offer.

Case and point to that fuel—Christian T-shirts.

Okay, I need the umbrella of grace here. I know there are some wonderful people who have the job of making Christian T-shirts, but it's time for some change.

I mean, why are vast majority of all Christian T-shirts lame?

For instance, why are most of them a knockoff of some well-known brand? I feel like I've seen every brand turned into a Christian message. I've seen a shirt that looks like it says *Reese's*, but instead it says *Jesus* written in the same font with the same colors. I've seen Subway, Sprite, Fender Guitars, Gold's Gym, FedEx, and the FBI all changed to some Christian message.

It's not Subway, it's *His way*. It's not Sprite, it's *Spirit*. It's not FedEx, it's *Fed up with Satan*. It's not Gold's Gym, it's *The Lord's Gym*, and one my all-time favorites: It's not Abercrombie and Fitch, it's *A Bread Crumb and Fish*.

At a white elephant Christmas gift exchange, I received the king of all Christian T-shirts. The statement on the shirt was, "That's What *He* Said" a reference to the sexual innuendo "That's What She Said."

Seriously?

Christian T-shirts are a microcosm of the Christian culture at large. In many ways, an alternative culture has been created and nurtured for Christians to extract themselves from mainstream culture and be able to maintain a similar but more wholesome version of staying hip.

It's a copycat attempt to stay culturally relevant by having Christian versions of rock bands, video games, fashion lines, breath mints, greeting cards, coffee shops, social media, and reading material.

Clearly, that is not all bad. In fact, having resources, entertainment, and opportunities to connect with other Christians has merit and benefit that we should utilize and support; however (and you knew there would be a however), we cannot allow this Christian subculture to be a place of *residence*. We cannot stay there. We can utilize the resources and environments created by the Christian community to refuel and enable ourselves to exist and contribute to the good of mainstream culture.

When the surrounding culture identifies the church through our flaws, our Christian celebrities, and by our T-shirts then we are not representing ourselves terribly well within the culture.

I mention the word *culture* because I want to explore some of the nuances of the American culture and the church culture. For centuries the church has largely influenced and shaped western culture, yet we are in a day and time that the church is rapidly losing it's cultural seat.

Think about history over the last two thousand years. The actual church building has often been the most elaborate structure in the city and often positioned directly in the center of the city. Until recent history, the church has been the single greatest cultural shaper in the western world. That's a fact.

Why the western world? In Acts 16 a significant moment occurs. Paul was stopped by the Holy Spirit from going east with the gospel and was told to go west. The east was full of strong cultures and weak governments. The west was full of strong governments and weak cultures. The gospel moved forward to shape culture.

The mission of God moved among the people around the Mediterranean for the next few hundred years then deeper into to Europe for the next thousand years. It then moved to the Americas, and finally, in the last hundred years, has found its way into Asia and deeper into Africa. Through the movement of the church, the culture has always been impacted by the gospel.

Today we have a culture that is changing in the west. The church, by and large, struggles to shape culture and is instead copycatting brands like Subway and FedEx to shape its own culture.

A Christian subculture is being formed that is forgetting how to exist within mainstream culture. Christians are losing the ability to bring the church into the center of culture, which brings us to Acts 17.

> While Paul was waiting for them in Athens, he was greatly distressed to see that the city was full of idols. So he reasoned in the synagogue with both Jews and God-fearing Greeks, as well as in the marketplace day by day with those who happened to be there. A group of Epicurean and Stoic philosophers began to debate with him. Some of them asked, "What is this babbler trying to say?" Others remarked, "He seems to be advocating foreign gods." They said this because Paul was preaching the good news about Jesus and the resurrection. Then they took him and brought him to a meeting of the Areopagus, where they said to him, "May we know what this new teaching is that you are presenting? You are bringing some strange ideas to our ears, and we would like to know what they mean." (All the Athenians and the foreigners who lived there spent their time doing nothing but talking about and listening to the latest ideas.)
> Paul then stood up in the meeting of the Areopagus and said: "People of Athens! I see that in every way you are very religious. For as I walked around and looked carefully at your objects of worship, I even found an altar with this inscription: to an unknown god. So you are ignorant of the

very thing you worship—and this is what I am going to proclaim to you. (Acts 17:16–23, NIV)

Paul was in Athens, the cultural capitol of the world, today's equivalent to New York City or Paris. He was looking to influence the city, but he is a visitor to the Greek culture. He understood that he must familiarize himself with the realities of the culture in order to have any voice worth listening to. As he listened to the Greek culture, it loudly screamed idol worship.

He was distressed.

How could he speak the truth in a culture so embedded with untruth?

Many authors and thinkers have marveled at Paul's strategy to engage the Athenian culture by inserting the consideration of one true God within the conversation of many Greek gods. He began by commending their commitment to religion and continued by inviting the people of Athens to consider the origin of the *unknown god* that they've identified with ambiguity. The altar to the unknown god acknowledged their uncertainty of the *truth*, and Paul spoke to their need for deeper answers. It's important to notice that he didn't come in to Athens with a bulldozer, tearing down the other altars and idols of worship, but instead he shed light on the one altar that provided questions and new possibility.

The church in America often feels that they have the right and the responsibility to tell people who and how they can worship in a public forum, instead of learning how to speak into a culture of many gods with new questions and possibility.

The points of connection to today's culture are not difficult to make. Today's society largely chooses to put their trust in things other than God. As a result, it is not a stretch to identify our culture in America as having similarities to ancient Greece. Our cities are not littered with literal altars of worship, but people are worshipping all sorts of things. I'm sure you are familiar with the list of usual suspects—money, sports, success, jobs, accomplish-

Idols of today's society

ments, sex, entertainment, fame, pleasure, esteem, popularity, leisure, relationships, greed, and the accumulation of better things.

How do we speak into that culture?

A culture, where in many ways…the church doesn't matter.

All cultures have the story of God within them, so it is a matter of finding the right avenues that will illuminate his story. Perhaps we shouldn't choose the avenues of picketing campaigns, or by making righteous lines in the sand that identify people as *in or out*.

Maybe we shouldn't count on our school systems to teach our children about our Creator. Perhaps hoping that our president will reclaim America as the Christian nation that some believe it was created to be is not the avenue we should drive down as intelligent followers of Jesus. I'm not suggesting we shouldn't pray for such things or care about them, I'm simply learning the gospel isn't dependent upon such things.

Let's consider the current landscape of the American culture. The American culture has some pretty defining characteristics:

1. *The American culture loves entertainment*—Movies, television, music, sports, and the arts.

2. *The American culture is consumer-driven*—We are addicted to purchasing what's hot. Give me a pet rock, Tickle Me Elmo, Teenage Mutant Ninja Turtle, Krispy Kreme donut, some Ugg boots, a North Face jacket, some skinny jeans, and an iPhone, and I should cover the essential purchases of the last few decades.

3. *The American culture idolizes celebrities*—We obsess over our actors, athletes, and political figures.

4. *The American culture is politically divided*—We fight over some issues. Thankfully not all issues (we need to recognize our similarities versus our differences in the political scene. Both sides might discover some pretty good things about the other).

5. *The American culture values success*—We believe in the American Dream!

Those are just some of the highlights. I have to be honest; for the most part I enjoy our American culture. I'll drop five bucks on a *Starbucks* coffee, I enjoy my MacBook Pro, I appreciate the arts, and I will spend too much money to watch the latest movie in IMAX. Why? Because I like some of the things America has to offer.

Culture is a good thing, but when you really look into our culture as a follower of Christ you have to ask yourself where are the themes of Jesus, the gospel, and the church? Where is the church in the story of our culture? And when we ask those questions the solution can't become to reestablish the church as an institution of power that sits in town square. Instead, the goal must be to learn how to speak into the culture as Paul did—by illuminating new possibility.

Culture is greater than the trends of fashion and entertainment. It's greater than the political climate and religious tension of the day. It's also greater than the value of the dollar or the state moral apathy. Culture is the story of a group of people. Culture is the ethos of a society. Wikipedia (a cultural icon itself) defines the term *ethos* as the Greek word meaning *character*, which is used to describe the guiding beliefs or ideals that characterize a community, nation, or ideology. The ethos is often portrayed through recurring and repeated patterns and practices of that community, nation, or ideology.

What is the character of our culture?

When I say, "Our culture," perhaps we should shift the perspective. Instead of pointing the finger at the American culture and characterizing all its flaws or strengths, let's take an honest look at the Christian culture and ask ourselves, "What is our character? What is our ethos?" If we can learn anything from Paul, it's clear to see that taking a bulldozer to all that has gone wrong in America will not help the cause of Christ. First of all, who defines the things that are right and wrong in America? Most would agree that scripture can inform us of such things, yet endless disagreements between faithful and scripturally informed followers of Christ reside in forms of politics, social policies, and Christian responsibility.

In order to accurately assess our Christian culture, we must first be introduced to the generation who is reshaping the American landscape of the church. Today's younger generation has many deeply embedded opinions about Christians, faith, and even Jesus. Maybe you've heard the term generation gap. This speaks to the differences between one generation and the next in the ways they think, work, what they value, and so on. Today's generation is experiencing a generation gap unlike any we've ever seen in American history, and there are reasons why.

We are living during an era of significant cultural shifts. This mostly has to do with the historical and philosophical shift called postmodernity. The term *postmodern* is an overused and often misunderstood term. I'll keep it very simple and leave the deeper explanations of postmodernity to the philosophers, sociologists, and historians, but for the purposes of this writing, it's important to realize that we are witnessing a historical shift in terms of major eras of time. There are certain markers throughout history that define certain time periods. Examples include the Greco-Roman Empire, the Middle Ages, and the Renaissance. Each time period was marked by major changes throughout the world either, economically, politically, or through innovation.

The most recent definitive time period is called the modern era, which lasted well into the twentieth century, with some suggesting its reign until the 1980s.[1] Since early in the twentieth century, we've witnessed the world changing at an immense pace. The advancements in transportation, communications, and technology are staggering, and as a result the world is different. It has led to the globalization of our planet in which the world is smaller and more united than ever before. These differences have created a historical shift and thus, ushered in a new era, the post-modern era.

The birth of the postmodern era has shaped new philosophies and ways of seeing the world. One of the most significant develop-ments has been postmodernism. *Postmodernism* is a philosophical movement away from many modern philosophies. Most notably, postmodernism adheres to the basic belief in no absolute truth but rather a relative truth based upon the individual's perception of the world. This philosophy has taken root in the postmodern culture of today, creating new challenges within the church.

This philosophy essentially says that you and I can determine different truth based upon our experience.

For example, if you think *Long John Silvers* is the best restau-rant on the planet based upon your experience, and I think it's the worst based upon my experience. Postmodernism, basically says both are true. I would say I need to take you out to eat. We need to expand your palette.

Therefore, there are two major ways to see postmodernity.

One, it is a historical shift in terms of periods of time, and two, it has bred new philosophies and ways of thinking that are becoming embedded within culture. Many in the church have identified these shifts as negative and are clamoring for the world to go back to the way it was. As you know, *the world does not go backward.* It only goes forward. These shifts are becoming cul-tural realities, and the church must learn to lead within them.

Many have called today's younger generation, specifically those born after 1975, the true postmodern generation (the Postmods so to speak). The implications of this historical shift have caused the Postmods to think differently about life and to value new things. Globalization has made the world smaller and smarter; therefore, this generation feels as if the entire world is at their fingertips. Culture is no longer centered in your hometown, but culture has become a global affair that has created a spiritual melting pot. Religions and belief systems are bleeding together, creating brand-new versions of spirituality.

So our surrounding culture is largely adopting philosophies that tolerate Christianity *as an option* for someone to believe in. Issues aren't black-and-white, rather faith is expressed in many different ways.

So what should the church do with this cultural reality?

Today's churches are attempting new strategies to connect with the changing generation. This is part of the reason we have churches that are so different from one another in this country. We have traditional churches, contemporary churches, liturgical, mission, video, house, and of course, we have mega churches.

Mega churches have probably affected the church culture more than anything. America has seen the rise of bigger is better! The last two decades America has gone from a handful of churches that would be larger than five thousand people. And as of 2014, there are literally several hundred churches in America that large and over one hundred churches that are over ten thousand.

So you would think with the development of large churches that the big "C" church is growing in the US but oddly it's not. It's shrinking.

Is it because everyone is leaving smaller churches and going to the bigger ones?

Maybe, but not likely. Even with the rise of mega churches, the decline of active attendees in a church is still shrinking in America.

The church is trying to figure out how to speak into this culture. But so much has changed so fast. First Church at the town square as the place everyone went has now become a wall of framed pictures and distant memories of the days when ministry was exciting. In the past couple of years, I've walked into church after church that had a *glorious* past, but a sad current reality of a body dying a slow and painful death.

Even in our young church we are experiencing all sorts of challenges to starting a church in an area of urban renewal. Years ago our nation and state created all sorts of legislation that was intended to protect the church from the *scary* prospects of an encroaching culture.

For example, years ago in Oklahoma a law was passed that prohibits bars (over twenty-one establishments) from being within three hundred feet of a church or school. This was created to "protect" churches.

The ironic twist to this story is that now bars are the ones being protected from churches.

In our search for property, we ran into all sorts of property owners that wouldn't allow us to even make an offer on their property because they saw the church as a potential liability to the renewal and growth of our city. They would rather save their property at the off chance a bar may someday want to be there than allow a church to preside there.

This was a hard pill to swallow. My belief is that the church is an essential ingredient to culture and the development of a community; however, many see it as a cultural liability and a deterrent to good development. I felt like we were often in an uphill battle fighting against all the stereotypes and preconceived notions of what churches were like. The truth is that most people believed that a bar would bring more life to the city than a church! And in many cases, they are probably right.

As a result, we began pursuing what it would take to create legislative change and give churches the ability to waive their right to prohibit a bar from being within the three-hundred-foot proximity. We also began pursuing a number of creative ways to help ensure the church could not only co-exist with any type of development, but that our church would be a significant contributor to the renewal of our city. We want our community to know that we will lead the changes necessary within our culture in order to share and speak a new story into our community. One that is not about separation, but one that is about inclusion, community, love, and respect. If it takes our church being a neighbor to a bar or club in order to share the love of Jesus shouldn't we be ready to do that?

The church in America is relearning how to operate within the changing postmodern culture. Some missiologists and futurists have already written the United States off as a lost cause. Stating that the rise of secularism and the establishment of post-Christendom is the nail in the church coffin in America. Comparing our trajectory to the course of the ever-shrinking church in Europe.

Although the fate of the marginalized church in Europe seems to be a blueprint for the future of the American Church, I refuse to lose hope for the United States, for Europe, and for the rest of the world.

So what do we do with this?

The natural instinct of many is to bear arms and fight the changes, to reclaim what feels like has been lost. The natural instinct is to get the government to protect our Christian values. The natural instinct is self-preservation. Many are fighting for the church in the name of restoring its cultural seat. A seat of power. A seat of institutional control. A seat of governmental persuasion.

Jesus never put his power in those seats.

Culture has changed...and it doesn't have to be a bad thing for the Church. We must pay attention and realize what message we are sending to the world around us.

> The church in America has become known
> exponentially more for what we are against,
> rather than what we are for!

How do we know this?

Mostly by listening to our culture.

Very Disturbing

Well over 70 percent of eighteen to thirty year olds (the Postmods) identify the church as judgmental, hypocritical, too political, out of touch with reality, and boring. In one study, only 16 percent of people said they felt like Christians consistently showed love to others. That means that 84 percent of people believe Christians aren't all that loving.[2] We want to scoff at such things. But it's easy to say that the church in today's culture has a mixed view. The church in today's culture has become largely irrelevant for many. The church doesn't matter all that much.

We may think, "Well, it matters to me and to some of my friends and to my grandparents, so it still matters!"

Yes, of course, it matters to some of us, but what about them? What about all the people that the church doesn't matter too? What do we do about that? Because there are more and more people like that every day. We have to carry the responsibility of why this increasing irrelevance is swallowing the church one bad T-shirt a time.

It's like this, the church is like a pineapple.

For me the pineapple has no competitors in the world of fruit. I feel like every time I eat a fresh pineapple, an explosion of flavor happens, and a party breaks loose in my mouth.

It's like I forget how good it is, and it leaves me wondering why I don't eat more pineapple.

Beyond the taste of the pineapple, the fruit carries some interesting traits that are worth mentioning for our conversation. Imagine never tasting a pineapple before and when you initially encounter the fruit, you are immediately struck by the shape and texture of the outside of the pineapple. When a pineapple is ripe, it grows a hard outer rind that is almost armor-like. It is covered in prickly spikes to fend off birds and other animals. If you were ignorant of what was inside the pineapple it may not seem worth the effort. It's intriguing, but it sends the message to stay away.

According to the perceptions of today's generation, the pineapple is an accurate picture of the church. Many people believe the church has formed a hard, rigid surface. For many, the church represents an institution that has dug its heels in on issues that condemn and isolate people. Christians have earned the reputation of being 'holier than thou' and judgmental—the perception is a hardened group of people that are close-minded.

Not only has the perception of the church become a hardened group of people, but many believe it has grown sharp edges that that are aimed at fending off anyone that may happen to disagree. People's questions are often answered by condemning accusations, or worse, people are told to clean up their sin prior to coming into the church. The reputation of the church has become a group of people that are not accepting, not loving, hypocritical, and judgmental. The message has been sent—Stay away!

Thankfully this is not all that the church has to offer.

We must learn to skin the pineapple. We must peel back the negative perceptions that have been formed and let them taste the heart of the church. If people can taste what the church was created for, it would transform the perceived character of our Christian culture.

> Taste and see that the Lord is good. (Psalm 34:8, NIV)

This generation, in which truth is relative to one's experience, is forming its perceptions about Jesus, but they've never even tasted the Lord. Postmodernism instructs today's generation to form its truth based upon their experiences. In many ways they aren't experiencing the church, they are experiencing the hardened outer shell of the church (our flaws, bitter Christians, close-minded spiritualists, etc.).

The church is misunderstood.

This generation isn't experiencing the Church, they're experiencing our Christian T-shirts!

✱ But the fruit of Spirit is love, joy, peace, forebearance, kindness, goodness, faithfulness, gentleness, and self-control. (Galatians 5:22–23, NIV) ✱

This is what the world must *taste and see* as the Christian community, but sadly, they often encounter the pineapple rind.

A few years ago a friend and I went to a University of Oklahoma football game. The football atmosphere for the OU Sooners is unlike many environments in the country. People become downright crazy-stupid about OU football. Many choose to make their pets personal mascots and name them Boomer and Sooner ("Boomer Sooner" is the classic OU chant) while others illicit greater disturbance by naming their children after the OU football greats. It is college football at its finest.

This particular fall day initially seemed like any other football game day. The 85,000 plus fans poured into the stadium ready for another probable win.

As we approached the stadium, we saw an individual carrying a sign. It was a rather large sign that had probably been constructed in someone's garage with a few pieces of wood, a bed sheet, and a bucket of red paint. He was walking by himself carrying a sign that said, *"This is of Satan."*

My friend and I looked at each other and then back at this individual, wondering if this guy was for real. Was he really standing on the lawn in front of OU's football stadium claiming what all these people were doing was of Satan?

We walked by him dismissing his possible delusional state of being, but we quickly learned this fella wasn't flying solo. We began seeing large bed sheet banners all around the stadium.

One banner read, "Repent and He will forgive you,"

Another said, "You are a sinner," and another said, "You're going to hell."

My least favorite banner I saw was carried by a guy riding a bike screaming at the people in the crowd as he rode by, and his sign read, "Jesus saves."

It angered me that these people had brought Jesus into their tirade on life. The mere method of delivery of the greatest truth the world has ever known nullifies the message. *Jesus Saves* wasn't communicated to the crowds; instead, judgment, insensitivity, being out of touch, hypocrisy, confusion, and hate were all communicated very clearly to the watching crowd.

It is a dose of reality to know that 85,000 people gather to watch football on Saturdays and park their cars in the nearby church parking lots, but only fractions of those people attend church on Sundays. Is it possible that only fractions attend because of the message we allow many in the world to see is of the crazy banner carrying lunatics that have confused their role in carrying out the great commission? Have we allowed the reputations of money-grabbing television evangelists, fallen celebrity pastors, lame Christian T-shirts, and the strange-and-out-there believers to shape the character of our culture?

I have a question for you.

What about you?

The majority of us aren't banner-carrying lunatics. We don't stand on the corners with bullhorns, and we don't have television shows asking for money. Do you have something to say about the character of our culture?

I hope you do.

I hope you choose to shed the hardened, sharp, outer shell the world is experiencing, and engage in the practice of leading people to taste and see how good He is.

Here's the overwhelming truth that we must wrestle with: in our everyday, going to work and school, living in our neighborhood, everyday life, we aren't terribly *different* than anyone else. Christians don't stand out.

We aren't different.

The postmodern culture is drawing conclusions about the church from the things they hear and see. Remember, postmodernism is a philosophy that adheres to truth being derived from experience. What are we letting our culture experience from us? Our religious rants? Our separatist attitudes? Our judgmental opinions? I realize that most reading this aren't the ones ranting, which means we are the ones who must help today's culture taste and see how good the Lord is.

America can't be our scapegoat of why Christianity is failing in our nation. It's not the government's fault or Hollywood's fault. We hold the responsibility of letting people taste and see how good the Lord is..

We must shift the perceptions.

Paul spoke God into a culture by humbly finding an opportunity to create a new conversation. We need to put the bulldozer in park. The answer isn't to tear down other things. Instead we must tell a *different* story.

Perhaps you've been wondering what this whole chapter about culture and the church had to do with living differently and doing things that matter. It has everything to do with it. We must live differently in order to change the ethos of the church in our culture. We must own the character of our culture and choose to *do something* about it!

You can be the most loving person in your neighborhood. You can be the most caring person in your child's school. You can be the most inclusive friend others have. You can be the most forgiving person in your family. You can be the most encouraging person at your work.

Perhaps your love for Jesus needs a little more volume in your life. Could you bring Jesus more front and center? Jesus shouldn't be a rare sighting in your public life; however, we don't need to put Jesus on display by wearing our *That's What He Said* T-shirt.

Maybe others see Jesus through the good we contribute, the words we speak, the help we offer, and the grace we show.

We must do better at the things that matter.

The story of the early church in Acts is incredible. They were scattered all over the region, and they changed their life for the gospel. They ordered their conversations about the gospel, they shared their possessions for the good of others, they endured hardship and persecution—all for the sake of the gospel.

They changed *everything* for the sake of the church. Today, we are sometimes hard pressed to ask Christians to change where they sit when they *come* to church. We are a far cry from the early church. However, the church is at the center of a life that is doing things that matter. Have you ever heard someone say something to the affect, "I don't have any problems with God. I just don't like church." There is a massive problem with this sort of statement because if you have a problem with the bride you have a problem with the groom. If you don't like my wife, but you like me, guess what? You and I have a problem.

With that said, I do understand why people say things like this. Many people have been hurt by someone in the church or have a sorted history of church experiences. Some people simply don't like going to church. Perhaps they don't enjoy the *church vibe*. There are many, many reasons I've heard about why people aren't fond of the church, but this is a skewed theology about God because *too many people think they can be okay with God and live without the church.*

Catch this: Where the groom goes, the bride goes also. You want to love Jesus? You need to love His church.

So how do we do better? What must change? It begins for many of us by deciding that the church will not get the leftovers in your life. Meaning whatever effort or energy you might have to spare isn't what the church gets. Of course, I'd say that right? I'm a pastor of a church, so obviously I'd love for you to give the best hours of your day to be spent serving the church, but remember, we aren't *just* talking about your local church (little c). We are talking about the being the church (big C). Being the church happens every moment of every day!

Being the church takes your faith from something that you've received, and it orders your actions and words throughout your day.

We are the church, purposed on this planet to live the gospel! So yes, we must be better at being the church. And yes, the church should be intertwined in the best hours of your day! Today's culture needs people who desire to change the ethos of our pineapple ways.

Maybe a few more of us need to have a simple, hopeful, ache in our heart to be the church the best way we know how.

Our culture needs you to tell a different story about the church.

Our culture needs you to live a different story of the church.

How to Allow people to see "Jesus" thru me in ways that matter:

1. Through the good I contribute
2. Through the words I speak
3. Through the help I offer
4. Through the grace I show.
5. Through having the church at the center of my life.

ৡৢৣ

Questions for Reflection And Conversation

1. What are some common challenges the church faces in your community?

2. How could the church tell a different story? Speak into the culture and into our communities in new ways? (Skinning the pineapple)

3. What is one way that you could live differently and as a result *be* the church (on a personal level) the best way you know how?

4. If zero responsibility is placed on outside entities (i.e., government, state-led academic institutions) what is needed for the church to matter in your community?

THE THIRD PART

LOVE RECKLESSLY

*What if we loved God and others with reckless
abandon and a selfless heart?*

CHAPTER SIX

Human Good

W hen I was seventeen I was in a car accident, which was regretfully my fault. As a result, I was issued a traffic ticket. The violation cited was *reckless driving*. I didn't even know what reckless driving was. The officer told me that it meant I was driving out of control without any regard for my own safety or the safety of others. Hmmm, I didn't realize I was even capable of that. I was required to pay a couple hundred bucks and attend driving school to prove to society that I would leave my reckless ways behind me.

The word *reckless* has stood out to me every since then. With a slight revision to the meaning of reckless that I was given, we can catch a vision of something beautiful.

What if our love for God and others was so out of control that we had no regard for our own self? What if we loved God and others with a reckless abandon and a selfless heart? What would happen if you became a person who loved recklessly?

These questions have led to a pursuit of becoming a person who does things that matter through our love.

Have you ever noticed how love is sort of a strange word?

Our definition of love varies between situations.

For instance, I love sports, I love autumn days, I love dough- nuts (yes, it's sort of a problem), and I love my wife. Obviously, there are unspoken ways of differentiating our love for our family and our love for our favorite foods, but the wide spectrum of the use of the word should be an indicator of our struggle to fully understand what love actually is.

The heart often symbolizes love. Every February, our grocery stores are filled with boxes shaped like *hearts* and filled with chocolate so every clueless and desperate husband can express his love to his wife. Nothing says I love you more than a cardboard heart box and four thousand calories.

Let's talk about the heart though.

The heart serves us as the organ most central to our ability to live. A heart keeps our blood pumping, our bodies breathing, and our minds working. A heart is also symbolic of our emotions. We say things like, "My heart is so full," or many of us have experienced a broken heart. The heart also represents what we hold most dear in our lives. Our dreams live in our hearts. So much about life is referenced or symbolized by our hearts, and love is best characterized as flowing from our hearts. Therefore, I believe we can conclude that as our heart is central to life, so is love.

So I believe it's fair to say that at the very least, love is complex. Case and point, my own love story.

Christie and I starting dating the summer that I turned twenty years old. From the onset, it was clear that this relationship was headed somewhere. It was not long before I was thinking that this girl could be the one. We enjoyed spending time together, we had similar interests, and amazingly she laughed at my jokes (that was a minor miracle!). It seemed like this relationship was moving beyond the go-eat-at-*Chili's*-and-catch-a-movie phase.

A few months into the relationship I was ready to muster up enough courage to say the big three words. I remember one night nervously looking for the moment to blurt it out. It's an awkward thing to figure out how to share your feelings. It's such a vulnerable and real place to be. The minutes were passing like hours, but finally I found my moment, and I confidently swept her up in my arms and looked straight into her beautiful brown eyes and uttered those three complex, scary, yet perfect words—I. Love. You.

Now I braced myself for her response.

What would she say?

Would she say anything?

I feared she'd simply say, "Thanks?"

I was relieved when she smiled and looked back at me and said, "I love you too."

Whew! Oh yea! We had fallen in love.

But, like I said, love is complex.

A couple weeks later, we are sitting in her back yard, and I could tell she was uncomfortable and that she wanted to say something to me. So she finally mustered enough courage of her own to say something to me.

She said, "I don't think we should say I love you anymore."

What? We had said it like two thousand times over those two weeks!

I thought that she was breaking up with me. I thought the romance was finished, kaput, over, done, terminated.

She went on, "I'm not breaking up with you. I'm just not ready to say that. Plus, I'm not sure I love you yet. I like you a lot though."

Hmmm, how do I take this one? I sat there shocked and feeling like a pretty big loser.

She took her I love you back!

Who does that? I was confused to say the least. My ego was in shambles, and my manhood was in a pool of shame at her feet (pretty sure she may have done a little dance on my pool of shame). Somehow I pathetically accepted these new relational terms hoping she'd love me back, eventually.

A couple months go by. Yes, a couple months, as in two, and nothing. She didn't say a thing about it. It was the massive elephant in a tiny room. She wasn't giving me an inch, and instead she said things like, "Boy, you are such a swell guy."

We were definitely planted in the *Chili's*-and-a-movie phase. At the rate it was going, I was considering a downgrade to *Taco Bell* and the dollar movie.

Finally, after three months I couldn't take it anymore. My shame was too deep, and my ego too fractured to let it continue. I had to initiate, to this day it drives me crazy that she made me come desperately to her feet again (but I'm glad she did). This time without much confidence but full of hope, I mustered the courage to ask, "Sooo…about this *I love you* thing. Can we say it yet?"

She casually answered, "Yeah, I think so."

Geez, that's it?

"Yeah, I think so."

She made me work hard for those words (maybe too hard). I'm so glad that she did though. It makes me love her so much more. I'm not sure if there are many things in this world worth greater effort or humiliation than love. Today, the love that Christie and I have for one another is still my greatest pursuit. I'm learning that I can never quit fighting and working for her love. Although she freely loves me unconditionally, I always want to pursue her. In a marriage it's easy to allow love to become something that we take for granted. Christie is the love of my life and taking her for granted would be tragic. I'm glad she took her I love you back. In many ways she taught me that love is way more important than three words and that love isn't an easy thing.

Oh and by the way, I hope our daughters take a lesson from their mom and make their future husbands sweat a little bit. It's good to keep them humble.

Love sits at the center of the *life* that we've been talking about through this book. Doing things that matter is full of loving acts, words, and prayers. A faith that relentlessly pursues Jesus seems to run smack dab into loving recklessly. His reckless love for us and the reckless love he calls us to embody.

A religious leader tested Jesus by asking him a question.

> Teacher, which is the greatest commandment in the Law? (Matthew 22:36, NIV)

In Israel, they *loved* the Law. The Law or Torah (as they called it) was deeply revered. The original scriptures, stories, and law were given to God's people in the books of Genesis, Exodus, Leviticus, Numbers, and Deuteronomy, and those five original books make up the Torah. The people often called the Torah, *the way, they truth, and the life.*

Hmmm, Jesus was up to something, wasn't he? It was everything to them. So Jesus, a new, powerful rabbi, who's kicking up a bunch of dust is asked to interpret the holy Torah and to share what he believed to be the greatest command in the Law.

> Jesus replied, "Love the Lord your God with all your heart and with all your soul and with all your mind." (Matthew 22:37, NIV)

His reply would have been considered a very good rabbi-like answer. That answer was taken straight from the Torah. It was actually considered one of the most sacred texts in all of Israel.

> Hear, O Israel: The Lord your God, the Lord is one. Love the Lord with all your heart and all your soul and all your strength. (Deuteronomy 6:4, NIV)

That was the first prayer a child in Israel would memorize. They actually had a name for it. They called it the *Shema (pronounced shah mah)*. Shema comes from the Hebrew word for *hear*, the first word in that text.

"Hear, O Israel." So this answer would have pleased everyone. Great job, Jesus! You've passed the test.

Then Jesus does something very unexpected, something actually quite staggering. He does a little freestyle with the Shema. He then adds,

> This is the first and greatest commandment. And the second is like it, 'Love your neighbor as yourself.' All the Law and Prophets hang on these two things. (Matthew 22:38–40, NIV)

What do you mean the second? The guy didn't ask for two. He asked what is the greatest, but Jesus adds a second and then goes ahead and states that *all the Law and the Prophets hang on these two commandments.*

These *two* commands?

This would have staggered those listening that day. Jesus is adding to the Shema—I mean who does he think he is? Who has the authority to amend the sacred Shema? Everyone reveres this statement, why is he messing with it? This is like me trying to add an additional tag line to Nike's *Just Do It* slogan. Consider me suggesting an addition.

"Just do it because of that doughnut you just ate."

That wouldn't fly. That wouldn't catch on. Not just because it's dumb, but because everyone already knows and says the phrase "Just Do It."

Don't try and fix what ain't broke. Surprise, surprise, I don't have the power to change Nike's slogan anyway.

Yet Jesus considers himself able to amend the Shema.

Is something wrong with the Shema? What is he doing here?

Author John Ortberg explains it like this, "Jesus, in an act of breathtaking authority and absolute brilliance, weds the notions of loving God and loving others together in a way that the world would be revolutionized by, and quite simply, would never be able to forget."[1] If you do not love people then you cannot love God. Jesus says this so often throughout the gospels that it has become known as the great commandment of scripture. Love is complex, deep, and multilayered, and somehow this thing called love is supposed to be central to what it means to be a follower of Jesus, but I think we may have a problem.

I'm not sure that we treat the great command like it's the greatest commandment. I have the conviction that *if love isn't easy, we don't give it.* Often we only offer our love when it doesn't require much effort. I wonder what would happen if we had an out-of-control type of love—one without conditions, fears, barriers, qualifiers, or protectors.

What if we loved when it wasn't easy or convenient? What if we loved God and others recklessly?

We can assume many things about the people who stand at intersections of life holding signs that read, "*Will work for food*," however, the truth remains that many of them are in need. I can't tell you how many times I've driven up next to one of these people and acted like I didn't notice them, acted like I couldn't see them. I've simply kept my head forward, hands at ten and two on the steering wheel, and just waited for the light to turn green. Years ago while sitting at a light and feeling the eyes of one of these individuals burning through my window, I heard a little voice from the backseat ask, "Daddy what is that man doing?"

Emily, my daughter, asked again, "Daddy what is that man doing?"

I didn't know what to say. Then she asked again.

Her words revealed my hypocrisy.

I chose to do nothing. I mean I didn't do anything bad. It's not like I ran into him with my car. I just did nothing.

James writes, "What good is it, my brothers and sisters, if someone claims to have faith but has no deeds? Can such a faith save him? Suppose a brother or sister is without clothes and daily food. If one of you says to them, 'Go in peace; keep warm and well-fed,' but does nothing about their physical needs, what good is it?" (James 2:14–16, NIV)

What do you do when different, needy, even smelly people break into your carefully protected life? What do you do when you're caught off guard and the stoplight can't turn fast enough or the conversation can't be dodged? What do you do when you are confronted with needy people, and you can't get out of the situation? I'm ashamed to realize how I responded. My love was empty and insufficient.

Jesus encountered situations like these many times. In Luke 7, Jesus is having a conversation with a religious leader and in walks a neighborhood hooker. She falls at Jesus' feet and bursts out crying. This would seem to be an embarrassing moment. Would people think that she was a prior acquaintance? She's not going away. She bowed in front of Jesus and begins pouring expensive perfume on his feet. Jesus is ready for the moment. He's not upset, uncomfortable, or protective of himself, but instead he sees and loves her in spite of her sins. He looks at her and says, "I forgive you, your faith has saved you. Go in peace."

Throughout the gospels, Jesus recklessly loves people outside the circle.

Erwin McManus wrote in his book *Chasing Daylight*, "We have defined holiness through what we separate ourselves from rather than what we give ourselves to. I am convinced the great tragedy is not the sins we commit, but the life that we fail to live."

I believe it's possible that many of us have made life much less about the love we are giving, and instead our faith, is about managing and reducing sins. Is this how we follow Jesus? McManus goes on, "You cannot follow God in neutral. God has created you to do something. It is not enough to stop the wrong and then be paralyzed when it comes to the right."

In order to love recklessly and follow Jesus we must be about action. It's not about being a good person with a low sin quota, but instead it is about moving into spaces where love has evaporated. The people Jesus loved were desperate hurting people.

In Mark 2 we encounter a story that teaches us what it means to love when it's not easy. This is a story about a paralyzed man and four men who encounter the love of God and its power when it is added to acts of human good.

> A few days later, when Jesus again entered Capernaum, the people heard that he had come home. So many gathered that there was no room left, not even outside the door, and he preached the word to them. Some men came,

bringing to him a paralytic, carried by four of them. Since they could not get him to Jesus because of the crowd, they made an opening in the roof above Jesus and, after digging through it, lowered the mat the paralyzed man was lying on. When Jesus saw their faith, he said the paralytic, "Son your sins are forgiven." (Mark 2:1–5)

We don't receive any background about the paralyzed man or the four men, but we can interpret a few things based upon history and drawing conclusions from other stories in Scripture. We must first identify that the paralyzed man is living in the ancient world. He has no wheelchair, and he spends his days on a mat. The world is not set up for him. He has to have someone help him move, clean him, and get him food. He would never experience any sort of independence; in fact, he would be totally dependent.

Someone in his physical condition would likely live as a beggar along the streets (similar to our two beggars in chapter 3) and similar to our modern day will-work-for-food intersection people of need. He depended on people dropping a few coins or food to him as they walked by.

No medical procedures can be done, and no rehabilitation facilities exist. He is seen as an outcast. He has no money, no job, no influence, probably no family, and seemingly no future. He does have one thing going for him, though—these four men. It's unclear if they are friends or simply men with compassion. It would be unusual for a guy like this to have any friends or people who would care for him. In the ancient world, people with physical abnormalities were the rejects of society. In fact, in ancient Greece, the Spartans would literally throw away babies who were born with physical abnormalities. They would take them out into the wilderness and leave them alone to die.

Truth be told, we all have our own abnormalities. They may not be physical, but we do have our unlovable stuff that we attempt to hide from others. Maybe your temper gets out of control. Maybe fear is your abnormality. Maybe you are selfish, or perhaps some sort of hurt is your baggage. Our abnormalities will eventually be seen. We all have them and have to deal with them. The paralyzed man can be any one of us.

For whatever reason, four men, possibly while on their way to see Jesus, decided that they must take this man to Jesus. They had heard the rumors of Jesus healing the sick, the blind, and the lame. Moving this man would prove to be a difficult task. They picked him up and carried him on the mat he was lying on. Likely, the men carried the four corners of this mat and headed towards the home where Jesus was teaching. When they arrived they immediately noticed that the house was overflowing with people. The crowd was so large that people were standing outside the house just hoping to catch a glimpse or faintly hear the words of Jesus. The four men and the man on the mat were not getting in.

I'm sure they were initially disappointed, but they quickly gathered and brainstormed together. Finally one got a crazy idea and said, "What if we knocked a hole in the roof of the house, and we lowered this man down to Jesus?" Apparently the cause to get to this man to Jesus was greater than any damage to the home or the effort it would take to make this idea happen. The men quickly found the tools they would need to lower the man on the mat through the roof. Somehow they climbed onto the roof while still carrying their friend on the mat. They determined the spot on the roof where they needed to make the hole.

Inside the house Jesus was teaching and the crowd was listening intently to his every word. While he was speaking, some people in the house began to notice pieces of dirt falling from the roof. The roof was likely made of some branches and tiles of dried mud. Suddenly, everyone noticed as more and more dirt begin to fall. Jesus stopped teaching and looked up as daylight shined through the roof. The packed house of people looked to the ceiling with wonderment then suddenly, a man on a mat was slowly lowered into the room. The room was completely quiet. People anxiously waited to see what Jesus would do. Was he angry at this interruption?

Imagine being the man on this mat. This was the biggest risk you've ever taken. Should you have trusted these men? What was Jesus going to do to you? What was he going to say? You could become the laughing stock of the house and of the town.

Finally, the man is completely lowered and laid on the ground. Jesus looked at him, and then he looked up at the newly created *skylight* and saw four faces looking down at him. At that point the scripture says something remarkable.

"When Jesus saw their faith, he looked at the man and said, 'Son your sins are forgiven.'"

This is one of the rare exceptions where we find Jesus responding to *their* faith instead of the faith of the individual. After Jesus said this, the paralyzed man picked up his mat and left. Completely healed, completely healthy. I imagine that the four men met him outside of the house and embraced him. They were cheering and crying and worshipping and laughing and shouting! They probably had a party and celebrated with the entire town over what Jesus had done.

That is reckless love. That is what we can be for one another. That is what we can be to the world. We can encourage, support, lift up, and cheer one another without any regard for the problems or abnormalities that others may have. We've all fallen short and need one another. We need people who are willing to see beyond the abnormalities of one another and do whatever necessary to get people to the feet of Jesus. Jesus recognized the four men's act of faith and love and he responded *through* it. Do we love like that? Do *you* love like that?

This is human good.

Once while traveling by myself, I was absorbed in some music blaring in my headphones, and I noticed a woman that was about to get on my plane. She was by herself, and she had what looked to be about an eight-month-old baby with her. She also had a stroller, a car seat, a carry-on suitcase, and a diaper bag. She had a lot going on to just get on the plane. I felt prompted to assist her but just before I offered to help, another woman stepped in right in front of me and assisted her by getting her stroller folded up and on to the plane. Once I was on the plane, I noticed her coming down the aisle and once again before I could spring into gentlemanly action, another man stepped in and helped her place her bags in the overhead bins. She sat down in the seat in front of me only to discover that she couldn't sit there because that seat didn't have two oxygen masks (one for her and one for the baby), so the person across the aisle kindly offered to switch seats with her. They switched and once she was settled in the aisle seat, the other person next to her (her new neighbor) asked if she'd prefer the window seat so the baby could look outside—he insisted she have it. They switched, and the baby loved the window!

Why?

Because human good exists.

It's sort of ironic that I noticed all of this, yet I didn't do anything to contribute to the good (sort of makes me feel like a lame duck). In this instance, God made me an observer of *life*. God was showing me something.

Human good matters. Doing good things matter.

If it's helping a mom in an airport or if it's handing a gift card to a person in need at an intersection holding a sign, it matters. Let's think about the cumulative affect of one act of human good per day. Let's choose the simple act of picking up a piece of litter we find on the road.

Does that matter? I mean it's just *one* piece of trash.

Let's make the piece of trash larger than a gum wrapper, but it's also not one of those random mattresses you see on the side of the road either (what is that all about). Let's average our piece of trash to being an empty twenty-ounce Coke bottle. An empty bottle weighs around seven ounces and is eleven inches tall. Picking up one bottle per day would equal a hundred and sixty pounds of empty Coke, Root Beer, and Mello Yellow bottles per year. If you stacked all those bottles on top of one another it would stand 335 feet in the air (the height of a large Sequoia Redwood tree). Let's say you did this one act of human good for forty years. Over that amount of time, the cumulative affect would add up. You would pick up over 6,400 pounds of plastic. That's over three tons of trash. It would also tower over 13,400 feet in the air (that's eleven Empire State Buildings stacked on top of one another and nearly the elevation of Pike's Peak).

Does that matter? Not to mention that recycling that plastic would save about 25,000,000 watts of energy.

So is human good about picking up trash?

Yes. But it's also about *all* the other good things that we can do. Clearly, we won't pick up the same piece of trash every day for the next forty years, but what about the cumulative affect of one act of human good every day? I have to assume it will mean more than a 13,000-foot tower of plastic.

For much of my life, I heard a specific statement within the church that challenges the concept that humans are naturally bent to do good. It's often said, "All of us are born with a sin nature."

There is clearly a theological understanding of this statement related to original sin and the resulting fallen nature of all humanity; however, I believe it can easily fuel an incomplete picture about our own identity. For a long time, the label of being a *sinner* gave me an excuse to sin. I mean, after all, I was born that way! It creates this ever-present disclaimer to why we are inherently *not* good. Something seems incomplete about this explanation of our nature and identity that we are taught at an early age. There's something inside of the natural behaviors I see in most people that tells me more about our *nature*.

Clearly, we *all have sinned*, and we all struggle with this battle between *good and evil*. Paul talks about it in Romans.

> So I find this law at work: Although I want to do good,
> evil is right there with me. For in my inner being I delight

in God's law; but I see another law at work in me, waging war against the law of my mind and making me prisoner of the law of sin at work within me. (Romans 7:21–23, NIV)

I certainly acknowledge, and personally experience, the war that happens within me. I'm not suggesting that sin and evil don't battle for our attention and even submission; however, what I saw with my own eyes on that plane tells me something different about humanity and so do many other experiences.

What is your natural instinct when a friend is hurting? To be there for them, right?

What about when you see a person accidentally leave their cell phone on the table at a restaurant? You pick the phone up and run them down, right?

How about when a child seems to be lost in a store?

Hopefully, all of us would stop and help the child.

Isn't the human capacity for good on display in times of chaos, terror, and tragedy?

My home of Oklahoma City has had its own dark moments through the years, and it has been human good that illuminated the way out. On the morning of April 19, 1995, I was in class. It was my junior year and about ten miles from my high school at 9:02 a.m., a bomb exploded in downtown Oklahoma City. Within a few minutes we started hearing the terrifying news. I remember going outside of the school and looking towards downtown and seeing a large plume of smoke and dust rising into the clear sky. The news that followed was not good. In the coming days we learned that our city had experienced a terrorist attack from a crazed militant activist that wanted to retaliate against the US government.

The stories that happened that morning of human good, heroism, and lifesaving efforts are overwhelming. Our country will never forget September 11, 2001 and the lifesaving efforts of the men and women who heroically charged in the World Trade

Center buildings when thousands were running out. My city will never forget similar stories that happened in the wake of the OKC bombing.

Tragically, 168 people died that day (19 of them children), and evil was there, but good was present in an even more powerful way. Over 12,000 people were involved in rescue and relief efforts in those few days. A spirit of love and pride to serve our city and help our fellow brothers and sisters was born in the ashes of the Alfred P. Murrah Federal Building and still exists to this day in the spirit of our city. Every since that day, Oklahoma City has been bonded by the human capacity to do good together. These days, I get our mail at the post office across the street from the site of the bombing, which in now the Oklahoma City National Memorial and every time I see it I am moved to be a better person. Thousands of people visit the memorial every year, and time and time again, I am told by those who go that they are inspired by the stories of human good that came from it.

Oklahoma has also had its dark moments courtesy of Mother Nature. Tornadoes are a relatively common thing for those who live in Oklahoma and 90 percent of the time they aren't a big deal.

But occasionally, they are.

May 20, 2013 was a big deal.

One of the largest tornadoes in recorded history tore through south Oklahoma City, the suburb of Moore, and other neighboring communities. The tornado measured over a mile wide and had a wind speed of over two hundred miles per hour.

I'll never forget a conversation I had with a friend who was a highway patrol man on duty that day. He shared the story of driving his SUV into the storm (rather than away from it). He said he stopped just a few hundred yards from where the tornado was about to pass over the interstate. He described the intensity of the storm and the black, ominous cloud that covered the ground. He watched as the tornado hit a bowling alley and picked up hundreds of bowling balls and hurled them through the air like cannonballs. Once the storm passed, he sped into the aftermath, driving over and through mounds of debris. He then worked for the next twenty plus hours. He said he lost count of how many trapped people he helped pull out of debris.

In the days ahead, thousands volunteered to clean up, help, and serve in any way they could. Our church was only a few months old, but we jumped in. Everyone felt compelled to *do something*. A group of us were in Moore a couple days after the storm and found ourselves in what looked like a bombed-out war scene. We were able to assist a few families over the next couple months. One of the families we helped had barely survived the storm. The mom and her two kids rode out the storm in their house. They didn't have a storm shelter or a basement, so they took cover in their bathtub. Experts say that if you don't have any sort of storm shelter, get in the tub! So that's what they did. Starla shared the story of laying on top of one of her kids and holding the other with her arms as the storm ripped their house apart all around them. The storm was so violent and so powerful that she could barely hang on to her daughter. I'll never forget as she told me the story of holding on to her daughter's hair to prevent her from being swept up into the storm. Her daughter was literally lifted up in the air and the only thing keeping her from being sucked into the storm was her mother's unrelenting grip on her hair. Then suddenly the wind stopped, and it was over. They were alive, but their house was gone, along with their car, clothes, fridge, favorite coffee mugs, and nearly everything else. As we helped them sort through the debris weeks after the storm and clean up what was left of their home, we thankfully were able to find a few pictures and keepsakes. We were honored and grateful to be one of the many groups, people, and organizations to help this sweet family try and get back on their feet.

The prospect of *not* helping was never considered. Why would it?

What makes people do this instinctively?

Why do people run into the darkness armed as the light?

Because human good is natural to us.

I would like to hear those who teach in our churches add to our comments and conversations about our *nature*. We've certainly all sinned and fallen short of the glory of God, but we were originally created for good. We also have a natural instinct to do what's right, to help when needed. We are certainly suspect to the temptation of evil, and we all fall into that temptation and do bad, but in my experiences with the world we are more naturally inclined for good.

Human good is all about love.

We can share, show, and give love to the people and world around us naturally and freely. Loving recklessly is about fueling what we instinctively know is right and good. When we act and follow through with loving acts, it will breed more and more loving acts of human good.

One of the best parts of the story from Mark 2 is after the men lowered the paralyzed man through the roof and Jesus had witnessed their act of love it says in verses eleven and twelve,

He said to the paralytic, "I tell you, get up, take your mat and go home."

He got up, took his mat and walked out in full view of them all.

This amazed everyone and they praised God, saying, "We have never seen anything like this!"

Who received the glory?

The paralyzed man? No.

The four men? No.

Jesus received the glory of the crowd watching. He's the one who did the healing. He's the one who did what no one else could do. It says that the crowd *praised God*. The four men did an act of good, an act of reckless love, and God added His love to their love and as a result, the people praised God!

Jesus says in John 13, "A new command I give you: Love one another. As I have loved you, so you must love one another. By this everyone will know that you are my disciples, if you love one another."

Our acts of love activate God's glory. When human good extends beyond giving when it's easy, and when our love requires sacrifice, effort, ingenuity, commitment, and a hope to get people to Jesus, it will be met by the love of God, and the supernatural can take place. The world will know we are *His* disciples through our love.

Jesus added to the love of the four men and made their effort and commitments to serve their fellow man a supernatural event. The men chose to love when it wasn't easy and to recklessly love beyond barriers, obstacles, and abnormalities; this *preceded the miracle*. When the love of the Father is added to our human good—our human love—we see the unlimited possibility of a *life to the full*.

Picking up trash matters. Helping a mom in an airport matters. Running into a storm to help others matters. Saying a kind word, sharing your resources, volunteering your time, serving your city, and helping the poor all matters.

Recklessly *doing* whatever it takes to get someone to the feet of Jesus—that matters.

Maybe that's why Jesus made that amendment to the Shema, because love matters.

Life to the full always pursues who God created us to be. Within your heart lies a person who desires to love. God's Spirit is pulling you and inviting you to become more of that person. The Spirit never guilt's you, shames you, or bullies you to become loving.

It compels you!

The years that we have left on planet earth are loaded with the cumulative potential to share a mountain of love and build ten skyscrapers of good.

Doing things that matter for forty years will matter!

The cumulative affect of loving recklessly changes the world.

It changes your life.

༄༅༄

Questions for Reflection And Conversation

1. Why do you think God ties loving him to loving others in the greatest commandment?

2. What about the four men from the story in Mark 2 most inspires you?

3. What is one act of human good you could do every day for a month? I encourage you to try this and measure the cumulative impact of consistently showing love in this way.

4. Who is one person God is speaking to you about to show love towards? (You may need to spend time praying and asking God this question)

CHAPTER SEVEN

Neighbors

M ost people who were born between 1965 and 2000 watched Mr. Rogers' Neighborhood while growing up. Fred Rogers was nerdy cool, before nerdy was cool. We all loved watching him enter into his house and put on his cardigan and white sneakers (they were incredibly white!).

He started his show the same way every time, all while singing:

It's a beautiful day in this neighborhood,
A beautiful day for a neighbor.
Would you be mine? Could you be mine?

It's a neighborly day in this beauty wood,
A neighborly day for a beauty.
Would you be mine? Could you be mine?

I have always wanted to have a neighbor just like you.
I've always wanted to live in a neighborhood with you.

So let's make the most of this beautiful day.
Since we're together we might as well say,
Would you be mine? Could you be mine?

Won't you be my neighbor?

Won't you please,
Won't you please?
Please won't you be my neighbor?

Fred Rogers obviously aimed at helping teach children about a variety of things. He talked about being a good friend, he took kids to see how crayons were made, he introduced you to mailmen and butchers, and you always took a trip to the Neighborhood of Make-Believe and entered a world of playful imagination. His show was on the air from 1968 until 2001 (reruns continued playing on PBS until 2008). His whole vision for a show began from a frustration by the way television was communicating and teaching children, so he did something about it, and it sort of worked.

His faith was no small detail about his life. He was actually an ordained Presbyterian minister. He was a devout believer and was passionate about what he did on television to portray the love of Christ through what he did. Perhaps that's why he elevated this theme and understanding about being a neighbor. He communicated that being a neighbor is a positive thing. He communicated that being a neighbor is a good thing.

Clearly, Jesus taught that being a good neighbor was central to our faith. Remember, he amended the scared Shema in order to elevate our understanding of what it means to love God. We cannot love God without loving people. I think most of us intellectually grasp this, but what about this word *neighbor*.

Do we treat Jesus's command to *love our neighbors* as part of the greatest command we have on our lives? Most people chalk this thought up to becoming a generally nice person. We live this passage by becoming a person who opens the door for the elderly at the Golden Corral, or asking our grocery clerk how their day is going, or making sure we give a friendly wave as our literal neighbors drive by us while we are doing yard work. We are smart enough to understand that loving our neighbor must mean more than that, *but* most of us aren't doing much more than that. What if we took this idea of loving recklessly to our *literal* neighbors? Perhaps we generalize the idea of neighbor with too broad of a brush, and we treat the idea of neighbors as *everyone*. As a result, we don't intentionally show love because when everyone is your neighbor often no one is.[1]

So let's get very practical.

How are you doing with the people who live on your street, in your neighborhood, in your apartment complex, or in your dorm halls?

Do you know them?

When was the last time you talked to more than one of them? How many neighbors do you actually know?

When that silent beckoning began whispering to Christie and I years ago about our *life*, one of the things we kept feeling God stir and give us vision for was a new way to be a neighbor. For the first eight or nine years of our marriage, we could easily say that the only neighbors we sort of knew were our next-door neighbors and even those relationships were relegated to an occasional and accidental conversation on the heels of mowing the yard.

So we began dreaming about what it meant to love our neighbors. It was an incredibly exciting thing to dream about. For us, the prospect of creating new friendships that lived on our street, helping our kids know other kids, and being able to subtly show them love captured our hearts. We dreamed that maybe we'd even be able to impact a neighbor's life for Jesus. It was so simple, yet the reality of it seemed so far from normal.

We dreamed with ease, but when it came time to actually be a good neighbor, it quickly became awkward and more difficult than it should have been.

How do you break the ice with a neighbor you've lived next to for years?

"Uh, hi, I'm your neighbor down the street. I've admired your yard for the last five years, so I thought we should officially meet."

That sort of conversation seemed so awkward, and fear wanted to keep me confined to my small plot of land in my neighborhood, but Christie and I had decided that we were committed to this, and we weren't backing down.

We decided that the only way to start this was to find ways that were natural to us. So naturally, Christie started baking cookies, and we started delivering them door-to-door. It's amazing how good food breaks the ice better than comments about their grass or the weather. We found that sharing with others was one way to open the door. These small successes of new conversations led us to keep digging into becoming better neighbors.

After a couple years of exploring and growing as neighbors, I heard Dave Runyon, author of *The Art of Neighboring* speak about this. He gave a compelling message about where to begin. His message was simple.

Learn your neighbor's names.

I'm embarrassed to consider how many times a neighbor had told me their name, and then later I forgot their name because of the *long* time that passed between conversations. What happens then? Well, when that happens, a universal reality happens— months down the road when you accidentally talk again, you greet one another with a holy, "Hey, maaaaannn!"

Let's be honest, your neighbors names are: Hey, man, Sup bro, Heeeyy, girl, Hey, you guys, What's up, yooouu, Heidy-ho, neighbor! and What up, dude!

Runyon and a group in the Denver area performed a study about how well neighbors knew each other. The vast majority of people knew zero to two neighbors' names, while less than 10 percent knew eight or more of their neighbors' names.[2] So the natural question is, "Why is this?"

Generally speaking, why don't people value knowing the people in their own neighborhood? More specifically why do Christians struggle to embody the greatest commandment to love our *literal* neighbors?

Like I said in the previous chapter, *if love isn't easy, we don't give it.* I believe there are a few cultural challenges that make loving our neighbors more difficult. In the past fifty to sixty years, neighborhoods have changed pretty drastically. Suburban America has changed the landscape of community and neighboring, possibly unintentionally, but nonetheless we have challenges as a result of *progress.*

Here are a few developments in the past five or six decades:

1. *Air Conditioning.* We spend more time inside our homes than outside thanks to refrigerated air. I mean, why sit outside with bugs and heat, when you have conditioned air and reality TV inside, right?

2. *Home Sizes.* In the past thirty years the average American home has grown from 1,400 square feet to 2,400 square feet, all the while the average size of a family has shrunk. So we have less people in larger spaces causing ourselves to stay more secluded in our miniature castles. We are literally becoming the kings and queens of our castles!

3. *Technology and Communication.* Sources of information about our community and the news of the day aren't discussed in town square or coffee shops anymore. Today there is an app for that. Information and communication are wirelessly accessed through our phone, computers, and televisions, which are all conveniently accessed from within our homes.

4. *Garage Door Openers.* Between the 1950s and 1970s, garage door openers increased with popularity and by the time the 80s rolled around, everyone had one. A great, progressive product, except a person can literally drive up to their home, open their garage, pull their vehicle inside their garage, close the garage door, go in their home, and never step outside of their home for weeks.

5. *The Slavery of Efficiency.* America doesn't suffer with many of the world's afflictions and great challenges, but I believe America is suffering in the form of efficiency. The speed of our culture is ever increasing, and people simply don't have time for relationships, therefore our energy

for others is reduced to an efficiency plan. Who deserves it most? That's the question we ask ourselves in order to prioritize our efficient plan of managing our relationships. Neighbors simply don't fit in our plans.

6. *Architecture.* It's funny how the design of a home can subtly turn families inward instead of outward. One of my favorite areas of our city happens to be where we live. The homes were built between the early 1900s up through the 30s. Homes used to be built with huge, beautiful porches. Porches that were meant to be used and lived on for relaxation and conversation. On top of that porches were built in the front yard, a convenient location to interact with neighbors. Today most new houses have tiny front porches that struggle to squeeze a few Halloween pumpkins on, and the backyard is where outdoor space is emphasized.

I'm not suggesting any of the above items are bad, nor do I believe they are a justifiable excuse for us, but it is obvious that some of the conveniences we enjoy have come at the cost of people naturally and easily interacting with one another. It's taken the cumulative effect of these things (among others things) over the last several decades to lead us to where we are today.

In the summer of 2013, a story hit all the news outlets about a group of kidnapped women who had been discovered. Two neighbors, Charles Ramsey and Angel Cordero, heard screams for help from a woman coming from the house next door. They ran over to the house and realized that the woman they had heard was trapped inside the house. They were able to successfully kick a hole in the door for the woman and her child to crawl out of her prison. Police were called and upon their entry into the house they discovered two other kidnapped women. The kidnappings of these women took place between 2002 and 2004. They had been held captive in this home until their discovery in 2013.

Another similar story happened in California in 2012. Neighbors were shocked to find out that a registered sex offender had held a woman and her two children hostage for nineteen years in a suburban backyard. When interviewed, neighbors cited that it was none of their business to worry about why he had tents and multiple sheds in the backyard, where he had been keeping them all those years.

In both of those cases, during all those years, no neighbor had ever made enough effort or had enough social interaction that may have alerted themselves to the tragedies that were taking place. Now am I saying this so you can go crack down on some kidnapping cases? Of course not, my assumption is that you have all sorts of wonderful neighbors that would be a lot of fun to know. My point is that most of us are disconnected and clueless from what *is* happening in the houses next-door or across the street.

Our culture has silently spoken about our neighborhoods. We value privacy. Don't be that nosy neighbor. As a result of those unspoken but understood cultural values, neighbors have become nameless faces that we know more about the cars they drive and their yard care habits than about who they really are.

I'm not saying to go and buy a pair of binoculars or to be an overbearing neighbor. My experience is that although our culture has built a perception of valuing privacy though our fences and nameless exchanges with neighbors, most people are actually very receptive to any neighborly efforts that are made. Most won't make the first move, but when a move is made it sparks forward motion.

So we started learning names.

We had broken the ice with cookies to our closest neighbors, but we needed to go a little further than just a few houses. We wanted to know our street. We started having the courageous yet simple walk down the street to strike up a conversation. When the conversation was over, Christie and I would immediately go and write their names down. We were committed to learning their names and actually remembering it. Writing their names down was the key for us. The next time we saw our newly named neighbors, we would greet them by name. Then the next time we saw them after that time we would *again* greet them by name. Amazingly this simple strategy sparked more and longer conversations. Knowing their names gave us more confidence to talk to them and in exchange I believe it gave them more comfort to talk with us.

Sometimes it's the simplest things—names.

Names eventually led to conversations and conversations led to invitations. We loved inviting neighbors over for dinner, but we really knew something was changing when they started inviting us! Eventually friendships were forming, and we weren't the only ones who wanted to be good neighbors. Being a good neighbor is infectious! Together with some of our neighbors we decided that we wanted to we throw a neighborhood party. Our first ever neighborhood party was a pre-trick-or-treating cookout in our driveway. We invited about ten households, and it was a pretty surreal feeling to watch this neighborhood that had recently been nameless faces to one another gather in my driveway.

It was such a simple thing. We had kids in costume, some cheap hot dogs, and everyone pitched in with some sort of side dish. We laughed, talked sports, talked life, played with one another's kids, and became friends.

Something about that season of life for Christie and I was so foundational. We were beginning to respond to that silent beckoning to do things that mattered with our lives, and in some ways, the simplicity of loving our neighbors was right at the heart of where God was bidding us go. Living the gospel isn't an illusive, philosophical, or ambiguous way to think and live. In some ways it's a practical approach to love our neighbors.

So what is the goal?

Is the goal to *reach* them?

Is the goal evangelism?

Well, let's consider this.

What if your neighbor never wanted anything to do with Jesus and through many efforts to present the gospel, they never received Christ. If your goal was evangelism then in some ways you would have *failed*. Our motive can't be to *reach* them. People can easily sniff out an agenda. Our motive can't be anything other than to love them. Evangelism certainly matters. Their potential relationship with Christ certainly matters; however, the goal shouldn't be to evangelize neighbors, it should be to *love* our neighbors.

Why?

Because that is the greatest commandment.

For the record, I believe in the Biblical mandate for the church to evangelize the world. Don't hear or think that I am minimizing the need for people to receive God's gift of salvation; however, when it comes to neighboring, evangelism has to be a natural outpouring of love.

Let it happen when it should, instead of forcing something that can potentially divide us from our neighbors. I'm sure *some* die-hard evangelists might say, "The way you love others is to tell them about Christ!" Perhaps, but our words are only strengthened and more genuine when they are accompanied by acts of love that demonstrate what we are saying. Our words are only more meaningful when a friendship of trust is built. Neighbors respond to neighbors who are neighborly.

The goal is to neighbor well.

> What if you became the most loving person in the neighborhood?

Christie and I asked ourselves this question as a sort of dream. We imagined becoming that type of person and family. It was during this season of stretching our neighborly wings that God clarified the overarching dream of our life to plant a new church.

Planting this church would require us to move into a new neighborhood. It was important to us that we lived and breathed in the specific area of the city we felt called. Missionally speaking it provided the *proximity* and *presence* that is critical when hoping to start a ministry that is incarnationally *with* the people who reside in the community around the church. That community was only about twenty-five minutes from our old neighborhood, but somehow it felt like a world away. The hardest thing about moving from our suburban home to a neighborhood in a diverse, unpredictable, more crime-ridden urban area was leaving our neighbors behind. We felt like we were just getting started with them, and we felt like what was happening among us mattered. On top of that, moving to new neighborhood meant new nameless faces.

It was clear that *loving your neighbor* was now a huge part of our life, and it would need to become a huge part of OKC Community Church. A few months after we began having weekly church gatherings, we began receiving all sorts of invites to be a part of all sorts of amazing causes in our city and other ministries doing work around the world. We were a new church in the area and as word spread about us, I found myself regularly having conversations with community and ministry leaders. I learned about all sorts of wonderful causes like helping women in crises, championing afterschool programs, engaging in the fight against sex-trafficking, serving those in need in various countries around the world, and serving campus ministries. The list could go on and on.

Honestly, I loved all of it and cared about all of it, but I struggled to sort through the needs and causes to determine where to begin. What should our church be engaged in? What causes should we serve?

I love moments of clarity.

When it seems like the stars align just for you.

For our church, we felt it was important to start with a simple yet profound cause. So many great people were inviting us to engage in meaningful causes, but I had to decide first things first. We had to build our foundation.

A few months after we began having weekly services, I shared with our church that we would have *one* cause and one cause only for quite some time. I explained that we would certainly support other ministries and organizations doing good work as we were able, but that as a church we were going to primarily focus on becoming certain kinds of people. Our cause, my moment of clarity, you've certainly guessed it by now—love your neighbor.

What if a group of people took that commandment and didn't just talk about it in an occasional sermon, but we cared enough about it to keep talking, keep pushing, and keep praying until we actually changed.

To begin, we encouraged our people to do the same first step Christie and I took—learn your neighbor's names and then see what happens. Our church has taken a hold of this cause. People in our church excitedly share stories with me about how they are building relationships with the people who they've lived next to for years.

So what about our new neighborhood of nameless faces? We moved into a neighborhood not far from downtown Oklahoma City and right in the zone where God had called us to plant. Since this area was part of the first residential ring that developed in our city in the early 1900s, it is a very eclectic and interesting area of relatively extreme socioeconomic, racial, and cultural diversity all within a small area. We love that our surroundings can teach our kids (and ourselves) how to relate to the wide spectrum of people that exist in our city. In the middle of all that is our simple neighborhood, that is quiet, family friendly, and perfect for us. Over the course of the first five months, we met about fifteen different households of neighbors on our street. We discovered we had all sorts of amazing new neighbors that we wanted to know more. During our first Christmas in our new home, we decided we should throw a little holiday *party* with our neighbors.

Let's talk about parties for a moment.

In Luke 5, we find a story about Jesus going to a party. The Scriptures say that a man named Levi held a great banquet for a large group of people. Like any party they ate and had several festivities. This was an unusual gathering of Jesus and his followers mingling with tax collectors and sinners. This dynamic created some unsettled Pharisees. Certainly an interesting scene.

In John 2, we find another story. This time Jesus is at a wedding. He was there with his disciples. The text doesn't infer that they were there to do some sort of specific ministry. It seems as if Jesus was simply there. He was likely a friend of the bride and/or the groom. John doesn't write anything about the actual wedding, but instead this story is about a scene that happens quite a bit of time after the ceremony. We know this because we read that the wedding guests had already polished off all of the available wine. Jesus's mother implores him to do something about the party that had just gone dry. Another interesting scene.

So Jesus went to parties.

It's funny how the word *party* has such varied interpretation. Depending on the conversation, it can be in reference to an innocent four-year-old ballerina birthday party. In other conversations it can mean an out-of-control kegger at a frat house. If someone says they are a partier, well, that likely means they are high as a kite. Sometimes the word *party* can even be classy, all you have to do is call it a *dinner party*. Clearly there are all sorts of parties: birthday parties, drinking parties, dinner parties, wedding parties, dance parties, work parties, holiday parties, pre-parties, after-parties, surprise parties, Super Bowl parties, tea parties, block parties, the republican and democratic parties, and the list goes on and on.

What about a church party? What does that look like?

Traditionally, a church party involves some potluck casseroles, a Jell-O mold, and if you're lucky some horseshoes for entertainment. That scene is all too often *not* too interesting.

We want to learn the *art of throwing parties*. Personally we want to do this, and we want our church to learn how to do this. Parties bring people together. They build relationships, and they create life. We believe that when we engage in life, we might actually find ourselves following the ways and rhythms of Jesus. Too many times in the church we try and systemize, categorize, and program life in order to shuttle people through our prescribed methods of community and discipleship. What if we decided to be more intentional about enjoying life with people?

Christie and I knew we could attempt to do this in our own life, but we wanted to encourage the people of our church to value parties as well. There is a purpose to parties. They aren't unnecessary "events." Instead they are *subtle attempts to reframe the way we understand the church and our faith*. Parties can help bring life to a city. We need to throw parties! I'm talking about bringing people together. It's crazy how many of us sit in our wonderful homes and think that our house is our escape from the world. Our homes should be quite the opposite of an escape. They are brimming with the potential to bring life and do things that matter. I believe our homes and neighborhoods may be the best place to build community and to recklessly love others. It can be the best place to enjoy life, enjoy relationships, and be the church.

We wanted to throw a party in our new neighborhood. Not with an agenda to get people to come to our new church or with an agenda to *reach* anyone. Our simple hope was to be good neighbors, to bring life to our neighborhood, and to build community. We teamed up with some new neighbor friends and together we co-hosted a Christmas party. We invited the twenty closest houses to us and hoped that they'd actually show up on a very icy December night (literally ice was everywhere). Walking on the ice was actually easier than driving, and since everyone was within a short walk, people actually came! We had about thirty-five neighbors crowd into our house, and we shared conversations, and enjoyed some great food and drink.

Those are some of life's greatest moments.

Moments where we connect.

After the party, my neighbor and friend Steven said, "That was one of the coolest things I've ever been a part of."

It was definitely cool. I watched neighbors who lived within a football toss from each other for years talk to each other for the first time. People exchanged phone numbers, reminisced about the changes in the neighborhood over the years, and together we dreamed about having more parties together. I was watching life being breathed into our neighborhood, and it was beautiful.

It's so simple, yet it's easily overlooked.

Jesus gave us a plan to experience life to the full and change the world. Love God and love others. More specifically *love god with all your heart, mind, soul, and strength—and love your neighbor.*

In order to help communicate our cause at OKC Community to *love your neighbor,* we developed a simple list of practical suggestions that are tried and tested tips on how to throw a neighborhood party. The list below is a conglomerate of our personal experiences and tips I've learned from others.

How To Throw A Neighborhood Party

1. *Get it on your calendar.* You have to schedule it or it will never happen. Schedule a time that is available for the majority of people. Sunday afternoon or evening is typically a good time, but you'll know best what works for your particular community. Scheduling around life events can work too (for example, a sporting event or seasonal themed party). Make sure you communicate the date and time to everyone with at least a three-week notice.

2. *Choose what kind of party.* Consider your neighbors. Are there several kids, older couples, or is it a mixed group? This may determine if you want to have an outdoor block party or an indoor dinner party.

   Here are a few ideas that work:

   • Rent a moon bounce for the kids, have a cookout, fire-pit party (roast hot dogs and s'mores)

   • Holiday-themed party (Easter Egg Hunt, pre trick-or-treating block party, Thanksgiving neighborhood feast [pot-luck style], or Christmas Party).

3. *Make nice invitations.* Make sure your invitations aren't cheesy, unprofessional, or unclear about why you are doing this. If you aren't skilled at creating graphics, it's worth finding a friend who can design a good flyer, or you can always purchase nice party invitations. It's good to know your neighbors names by this point in order to personalize the invite. Somewhere on the invitation say something such as, "We think it's about time to know our neighbors!" People want to know your intentions, and people like to be invited to nice events. When passing out the invites do your best to hand deliver them, in order to create a connection with your neighbor about the purpose and hope for the party.

4. *Be inclusive.* Invite a large group of people. This will avoid the impression that you are being exclusive. Inclusivity is important! It also gives you a much higher chance for success. This being said, you still need to know where to stop. Use the geography of your neighborhood to find natural stopping points like an intersection or other landmarks that helps create an understandable divide.

5. *Food is the icebreaker.* Food is always a good way to bring people together. It also serves as a great way to break the ice as people arrive and begin mingling.

6. *Allow conversations to be the centerpiece.* Don't over plan. If you have food, you won't need to prepare entertainment. Allow conversation to be the centerpiece of your time. Only prepare a brief introduction (if you feel it necessary) to the time together to welcome and get conversations going. Depending on the party, you might have to organize some simple games or activities, but do your best to keep the environment very relaxed.

7. *Involve others.* See if anyone would like to help prepare and/or provide for the party. Involve them in the food needs (most people love to help). This helps ensure that they will be there and feel more invested. This is less about *you* throwing a party, and more about *we* are having a neighborhood party.

8. *Be transparent about your life.* People may be curious as to why you initiated the party. Feel free to share that knowing your neighbors is something that you value and that you desire to have a strong community within your neighborhood. Simple and honest statements or stories about your hopes and desires for deeper relationship will inspire others. You may even feel led to connect this desire to your faith.

9. *After your first party.* Once you have a party, you and your neighbors will likely want to have another. Consider a different neighbor hosting it at their house or yard, so it becomes more collaborative and owned by everyone.

Learning names.
Throwing parties.

Those are fine and good things, but when you do those things *because* of your heart to live and embody the greatest commandment to love God and love our neighbors, it will eventually lead to moments where your neighbors ask you for help. You'll become the person they call to water their flowers when they are out of town, to keep an eye on things for them, or watch their kids for thirty minutes while they run an important errand (you're thinking do I want that? Trust me you do!). Those nameless courtesy waves that used to be the norm turn into conversations about life. Remember, being a good neighbor is infectious, so the neighborhood changes, and they'll help you when you need it. People will know one another, look out for one another, have meals together, share tomatoes and watermelons from their gardens, and enjoy life together.

In our house we are pursuing this greatest commandment thing because it seems rather important! We have confidence that God is working in us and through us as we seek to become people who love our neighbors. Neighbors may not become the most important people in your life (I'm not suggesting they should be), but they should become people who are *in* your life.

I think it's fair to say that many of us who think we *love our neighbors* actually live more reflective of Mr. Rogers' *Neighborhood of Make-Believe,* and it's time to get honest about what's real and what's not. We don't know our neighbors, and even if we do know a few names, the truth is that we don't thoughtfully or prayerfully consider what it means to recklessly love the people who are literally right in front, around, and next to us.

Love. Your. Neighbor.

A simple, hopeful, and beautiful way to be human.

❧❧❧

Questions for Reflection And Conversation

1. How many neighbors do you know by name?

2. Dream for a moment. Who in your neighborhood, apartment complex, dorm hall, or surrounding community could you begin living out the greatest commandment with? (Perhaps, by starting to have conversations with).

3. Dream for another moment. If you chose to take a swing at throwing a party, what could it look like?

4. How could intentionally loving your literal neighbors stretch you as a Christ follower and be full of all sorts of things that matter?

THE FOURTH PART

LEAD COURAGEOUSLY

What if we never allowed fear to stop us? Ever.

CHAPTER EIGHT

Leading Isn't About Leading

I remember pulling my daughter Emily aside when she was about six years old after an argument between her and her younger sister Carys. I decided that it would be a good moment to talk about leadership and being a good example for her sister to follow. I imagined a meaningful moment that would inspire Emily to new heights. I shared with her how she needed to be a leader to her younger sister, and I talked to her about the power of her influence.

I remember actually saying, "Now, Emily, your mommy and I are both leaders, and we want you to grow up and be a leader too."

This is inspiring stuff here, right? She began to tear up, and I could tell these weren't tears of inspiration, so I asked, "What's the matter, Emily?" She looked at me and said, "Daddy, I don't want to be a leader when I grow up. I want to be a photographer."

Too much too soon?

No matter what we want to *do* once we grow up, whether we become a photographer, a scientist, or a teacher, we all are given the opportunity to lead. Leaders are everywhere and do all sorts of things. I've met incredible leaders who are college students, financial advisors, stay-at-home moms, nurses, small business owners, and non-profit pioneers. Leaders take whatever they do and *do things that matter* with it. I believe there is a turning point for every leader where leading is no longer about simply trying to influence others, but leadership becomes very much about courage.

Courage in its purest form is the willingness to conquer fear. Courage is assigned to many things in this world. It is often associated with being a daredevil. People who jump out of planes, walk across high wires, hurl motorcycles in the air while holding on, and wrestle crocodiles are considered full of courage (possibly considered crazy too). We can agree that it takes some form of courage to do such things, but is that real courage or is that just crazy?

Have you ever really been afraid? Has something ever *really* scared you?

Possibly my greatest moment of fear happened in the ocean.

I was leading a team of high school students on a mission trip in the Houston area, and we took one afternoon and headed to the Galveston beach. Now the Galveston beach isn't exactly a tropical haven. The water has more of a brownish/blackish/greenish tint and the beach is, well, it has sand. Nonetheless, it's the ocean, and it has waves, so we were getting in.

After being in the water no more than ten minutes, I decided to head back to the luxury of the Galveston beachfront. As I'm walking out of the water, all the sudden I felt something under the water grab my foot.

I immediately felt intense pressure around my back of foot, like something clamped down around my lower ankle. I immediately leapt as high as I could and started kicking my legs. I believe I said a few words that weren't acceptable on the mission trip code of conduct agreement. Later I found out that if something grabs you under the water in the ocean, you are free to say whatever you want, so I'm good. Then I looked down to see what had happened, but remember I was in Galveston and I couldn't see through the murky drudge of ocean water. So I ran out of the water and I looked down at my foot and blood was rushing out of the inside of my foot, right below my ankle.

I looked around, but no one had noticed my tangle with nature. At this point I had no idea what it was. I thought maybe it was a large crab, but it seemed unlikely due to the intense pressure. I cleaned the wounded area up and was surprised to see that it was only one very deep hole in my foot.

I'm thinking, *What would leave one puncture?*

I couldn't think of any one-toothed sharks.

A few in my group noticed the blood and were now interested in what had happened to me, so we began contemplating the possibilities. About ten minutes after the incident, my foot started burning and an immense amount of pain began to shoot through my leg. A friend of mine jumped on his iPhone (thank you God for the iPhone), and he quickly started Googling some possibilities and found a picture that looked exactly like the hole in my foot.

He showed it to me and said, "You were stung by a stingray!"

A stingray? Those things have been known to *kill* people. I came to understand that I had likely stepped on the stingray and its tail wrapped around my foot, and its barbed, poisonous stinger stabbed me in the inside of my foot. When it stabbed me, it created such pressure it felt like something grabbed my entire foot. My friend continued to read, "There is very little you can do for the pain."

Bummer.

He went on to say, "You need to prepare for extremely intense pain for the next three to four hours"

I hate you, iPhone.

I think I had about five people say they were willing pee on my foot to help with the pain. I guess that's rumored to help. I passed. As the pain began to increase, I decided I didn't want to hang out on the luxury of the Galveston beach any longer while everyone sat around and stared at me, so I went and sat in my car the rest of the afternoon. I sat in my vehicle, writhing in pain for the next four hours while my teammates splashed in the black water.

Since that experience I've been back to the ocean and it's an exercise of courage every time I enter the water, because I wonder, *What if he's in there, waiting to finish the job that he started?*

Courage is exercised in the endless circumstances throughout life. Beyond moments of overcoming fears like man-hunting stingrays, I believe we mostly associate courage with the heroic moments of men and women doing things to risk their safety for the well-being of others. Things like running into a burning building or being a soldier on the battlefield. Clearly it takes courage to do those things, and those people are worthy to be titled courageous.

There is a type of courage, however, that will never make the headlines. It will never be filmed or talked about much, and it's not a story that takes place on Mt. Everest or in an ocean battling the world's deadliest beasts.

It's a type of courage that people like us can live with.

I believe it's in the unpublicized moments, in the midst of routine days, and in the lives of people like you and me where the most important battle over courage gets waged.

> For God has not given us a Spirit of fear and timidity, but of power, love, and self-discipline. (2 Timothy 1:7, NIV).

He has given us a spirit of power, yet often we succumb to the emotion of fear. My theory is this: *the biggest hindrance to leadership is fear.* Fear often stops us dead in our tracks and paralyzes us from actually doing the things that truly matter. Fear is an emotion we all have. A healthy fear of God leads us to faithfully obey and follow him; however, the fears we often live under are the ones that hinder us from actually following God. These fears are evil.

One petty and irrational fear I have is birds. I don't mean little birds sweetly drinking from a birdbath or flying through your backyard. I don't mean cardinals perched on a fence, tweety birds, or parrots (although *talking* birds should freak us out).

No, what I fear is big masses of birds that can attack you if they want. When I was a kid I watched the Alfred Hitchcock flick, *The Birds,* and it messed me up. The birds in that movie were demon possessed! I have considered the possible realities of that movie and made some sobering conclusions. I've realized that if birds ever figure out that they outnumber us a thousand to one, they could unite and take us out (thank goodness God gave them tiny brains).

Beyond the petty fears we all have lay other, more personal, fears that create pause in who we are and what we could be. They stop us from becoming who God created us to be. In order to fully engage the discussion of doing things that matter and leading courageously we must pause.

Because leading isn't really about leading.

Let me explain it like this. One of the most pampered experiences of my life was on a cruise ship.

Endless food, exquisite service, and the royal treatment.

If I thought life was like a cruise ship, I would be grossly misunderstood. If I thought life would be chocolates on my pillow and iced-tea delivered to me on a silver platter as I lay by the pool, I would be oblivious about real life.

Life is different than the silver platter lifestyle of the cruise ship.

Likewise leadership is different from the silver platter version of leadership that schools, churches, and parents have called young people to. Within those arenas of life, leadership is brought out on a silver platter, and all one must do is what they are told. The underdevelopment of leadership during the younger years of life has led to puny leaders later in life who stop short of doing anything that matters.

So what is silver platter leadership?

Well, it's what most people call leadership.

- It's being involved.
- It's thinking that leadership is about working hard.

- It's identifying leadership by attendance.

- It's surrounding yourself with people who are easy to lead.

- It's leading when there is no opposition.

- It's showing up when you can.

- It's being the team captain (it's a luxury to be celebrated).

- It's reading leadership books.

- It's having a title or a position.

The above list isn't full of bad things. In fact, some of these things are good; however, this is the easy part of leadership. Hopefully we show up on time, read leadership books, work hard, and are involved. It just can't stop there.

You see the silver platter side of leadership

It is safe.

It's comfortable.

It's easy.

It's where the majority of leaders stand on top of their conquered mountain feeling like they've arrived. We will lead when courage is not required. We will lead when adversity doesn't exist. We will lead in the friendly confines of the church, the student council, or the neighborhood association (all good things). We choose to lead in environments that are safe and where leadership is encouraged and it's virtually impossible to fail. But when leadership *requires courage;* something different is poised to happen. The power that Paul talks about in 2 Timothy is ready to be unleashed and God is ready to move.

Our fears will get in the way of God moving. There are four primary fears that paralyze us from leading courageously.

- *Fear of the Unknown.* We fear what we don't know. We ask ourselves, *if I step out what will happen to me? If I take the step down this road, I don't know where I'll end up.* The fear of not knowing what lies ahead often causes us to stall, and we end up sitting at the intersections of life fearful about what to do.

- *Fear of Failure.* What if you fail at what everyone expects of you? What if you stepped out and tried to lead and it didn't work? The fear of failure stops us from ever taking the risk of what could be or even what should be because we desperately avoid failure. Giving yourself and those around you the freedom to fail is the most empowering thing you can do to encourage courageous leadership.

- *Fear of Rejection.* No one enjoys the feeling of another person's rejection. Leadership rooted in following Jesus will result in rejection along the way. It just comes with the territory. When you step down the road of courageous leadership, you will face opposition. People you care about will turn their back on you. Allow yourself to be esteemed in new ways and by new people.

- *Fear of Losing Something.* What if you had to abandon personal desires and dreams? If you do what God is calling you to do it will likely cost you something. The road of courageous leadership will always cost us something.

Other fears exist, but the majority of our fears fit under the umbrella of one of these four. Chances are you are currently submitting to one or more of these fears in your life. Remember what Paul wrote, *"For God has not given us a Spirit of fear and timidity, but of power, love, and self-discipline"* (2 Timothy 1:7, NIV).

We must lead beyond the silver platter and step into His Spirit of power and love and self-control.

There will be situations you are not ready for. You will have to make tough decisions. You will have to dig deeper into your faith. You will have to forge new ground. You will have to make bold steps and trust where God is leading you. It is in your fears and subsequent submission to the Father that we find true strength.

Imagine becoming a person who leads beyond the silver platter and becomes a courageous leader who is faithfully doing things that matter.

But like I said, leadership isn't really about leadership.

What does that even mean? Well, first of all, leadership is about courage, not leadership. Secondly, and possibly most importantly, leadership is not leadership, rather it's about, well, before I tell what *secondly* is, let me tell you a story.

One of the most traumatic experiences of my life occurred at the tender age of six. My family lived in West Germany.

Yes, I said *West* Germany (an actual country from 1949 to 1990).

It was 1984, and the Berlin Wall was still standing strong as the symbol of the Iron Curtain and Cold War that existed between the United States and the Soviet Union. Thankfully, at six years old I was unaware that a mere few hours away from our home was our nation's greatest threat.

A few hours the other direction from where we lived was the majestic city of Paris, France. Although I was young, I still vividly remember our trip to Paris to visit the Eiffel Tower, the *Louvre* museum, and the other iconic landmarks scattered throughout the city.

(Possibly the memories were the reason I later chose Paris as the honeymoon destination for Christie and I—that or the fact that I found a great deal!)

It was on my family's trip to Paris at six years old that my life was jeopardized. My family was walking through the *Louvre* museum courtyard, which is a wide-open space. I was walking about ten or fifteen feet behind my parents, and in between my parents and myself were my two sisters, Sally and Katie. Sally, who is my oldest sister and eleven at the time, was walking closest to me. As we were strolling across the courtyard and breathing in the Parisian culture, something happened.

I was taken.

I was literally grabbed, picked up, and immediately carried away. My mind was confused.

What was happening?

Two men had picked me up and were quickly moving across the courtyard. The men were speaking to each other, but they weren't speaking English. I remember crying out and seeing Sally turn around to watch me being taken away. Initially she stood there frozen and uncertain of what to do. She began to yell to my parents, who were now farther away from us. I was seriously being kidnapped in Paris! I'm pretty sure I've seen movies starring Liam Neeson that were about this kind of thing.

It all happened so fast. I could only hear Sally yelling, but I could no longer see my family. I was clearly terrified. All of the sudden we stopped. I was no longer being dragged across the courtyard, and I found myself surrounded by a large group of people. I looked around, and at least twenty people were speaking in a foreign language and smiling at me while pointing for me to look ahead. Before I could process the moment in my little six-year-old brain, a dozen cameras flashed, and in a split moment, the crowd scattered and I was gently shoved back on my way. As quickly as it had happened, it ended.

My parents came to my rescue just in time to see me nervously standing alone while the perpetrators scattered. They barely realized what had happened. Sally was the only one who had seen the ordeal, so she seemed to sympathize the most with my brush of terror. As I pulled the moments together in my mind (with the help of my parents), I realized that I had been the victim of an overzealous Japanese tourist group that saw a chubby white kid and likely determined that I was the perfect French boy for their photo op. I'm sure they imagined I would be perfect for their albums and slide shows upon returning home. I hadn't been kidnapped, but instead I was simply a prop for a Kodak moment. To this day I occasionally wonder if I am in a photo album of some couple's unforgettable trip to Paris. The Parisian kidnapping of

'84 was nothing more than a group of camera-happy tourists whose desire to capture the moment was bigger than their brains.

Things aren't always what they seem to be.

It all happened so fast, and for a brief moment, I truly believed I was being kidnapped. We've all had moments in life where we believed something to be true only to later learn the real truth. As a kid, I was told that if I swallowed apple seeds I would have trees start to grow inside of my stomach and eventually apples would grow out of my ears.

Call me stupid, but this freaked me out!

At age five or six years old, I recall seeing a mysterious shadow in the hallway outside my bedroom on Christmas Eve. I promise you, that it looked like a large man with a puffy beard and a hat.

Things aren't always what they seem to be.

Possibly we can categorize these moments as misunderstandings, assumptions, accidents, ignorance, or misinformation. Whatever the reason for the miscalculated truth, it still remains that we have lived for moments or years during our life believing in something that was not true. I can think of religious beliefs I once held that were taught to me by my church during my younger days that today I simply don't believe are true or even biblical.

Leadership may be the most misunderstood subject in today's world. It may also be the most talked about, studied, and over defined subject in the world. Many people claim to possess the varying qualities that define leadership and nicely line them up in bullet points on a resume. If the world housed as many leaders as are self-proclaimed, the world would be a much better place than it actually is.

Leadership is not always what it seems to be.

Countless books, blog posts, sermons, conferences, and staff meetings have tirelessly tried to right the mistakes of misinformed definitions of leadership. The problem with all of those mediums is not the audience or the messenger.

Rather the problem is the reality we live in.

Leadership is defined every day by the way we harness it, practice it, pursue it, and share it. Our written definitions inform and inspire us to be better but again, leadership is defined by the way one lives it.

Simple conclusions from practiced and lived out definitions of leadership in our world inevitably informs us that leadership is often about *power*. Many would like to sugarcoat this particular observation by pointing to the many examples of servant leadership that are expressed or the varying qualities that point to leadership being about empowerment or vision and although worthy examples exist, they seem to be exceptions rather than the rule.

I imagine the word *power* elicits a myriad of thoughts for you that range from images of political power, business tycoons, media, Wall Street, and even the power of God. The American Dream is riddled with this desire for power. Many identify the American Dream as a pursuit of fame and fortune, which is always accompanied by power. Every year Forbes magazine creates a list of the world's most powerful people. Why do they do that? Because the world believes power is important. Power is the gateway to being somebody that matters. The list is littered with the world's most powerful politicians, business moguls, and even famous entertainers (for example, Oprah has consistently been a member of the top one hundred). Even the founders of Google, Larry Page and Sergey Brin, have cracked the top ten a number of times, proving that *knowledge is power* (I Googled the list).[1]

It is difficult to admit, but we all seek power. We need power, we crave it, and when we don't have it, we fight for it. The word *power* conjures up mixed reactions. On one hand, we see its purpose and potential for good, and on the other we see its danger and potential for abuse. We've witnessed those who seek power for the sake of holding positions, authority, and recognition, and most of us tell ourselves that we are not one of those power hungry individuals in it for selfish reasons.

Do you enjoy having power?

That may be an unfair question. We all want to have some level of power over our lives, and possibly, even authority over the environments we find ourselves in, and I don't believe that is a bad thing. Power isn't bad, but it's the methods enabled to achieve the power that typically lead us to become people who are living miscalculated definitions of leadership. The hunger for power begins early. Watch any interaction between children playing with toys. What is going on? A dance for domination and the survival of the fittest for that block, racecar, or Barbie doll is at stake. An outburst of hitting, biting, screaming, crying, and Band-Aids can become the results of the power struggle among children.

As we grow older, the reach for power exists in the forms of the cutthroat world of business where we must either kill or be killed. It exists in the symbolic ladder of success, which requires you to look out for number one. The pursuit of power is alive in political smear campaigns, which look to devour the opponent. We can smell it when talking to a friend who always has the better story and the latest gadget. They are the king or queen of the one up. Having the upper hand is perceived as intelligent leadership. Placing yourself in a position of power is respectable and understood to be freeing under the standards of the world.

Is leadership about power? Seemingly those who have the most power are believed to be the best leaders. Power has long been the mark of leadership. This is why we study powerful rulers, conquerors, and entertainers throughout history. I dare say, *things aren't always what they seem to be?* Maybe becoming a leader who does things that matter has nothing to do with all this leadership talk that is flooding our world. What if we actually lived a different definition of leadership?

I often feel surrounded by poorly lived definitions of leadership. I often feel that I embody poorly lived definitions of leadership.

In John 13, Jesus redefines leadership through his actions.

Jesus and the disciples had entered Jerusalem after three years of powerful and world-changing experiences. The story in John

13 happens within days of the disciples arriving in Jerusalem. Their arrival took Jerusalem by storm. The people of Jerusalem welcomed Jesus and his disciples by laying palm leaves along the road they traveled, all while singing and praising Jesus as king. Can you imagine the emotion and pride of the disciples? I'm sure they felt like they were a part of the most significant thing the world would ever know. Certainly the gravity of these moments could not fully sink into their hearts, but they must have recognized the overwhelming privilege they had been given by the Lord.

The disciples didn't understand what coming to Jerusalem would mean. They were in the final days of Jesus's time on earth. The story we read in John 13 is in the final hours preceding his betrayal and arrest. The scene is the infamous last supper. Many of us have a movie-set image in our mind of a scene with Jesus sitting at table filled with fruits, breads, and wine while his disciples gathered around intently listening to their teacher.

Let me paint a deeper understanding.

It is believed that Jesus and the disciples met in a place called the Upper Room. Although Jesus had entered Jerusalem days earlier as a hero, the mood in the city had changed. He and the disciples were now in danger and needed a safe place. The Upper Room became the first meeting place for the early church (Acts 1). This room was literally an upper room in a house. We can assume that it was a large house because in Acts we learn that 120 people gathered in it. In the room on this particular night a table had been prepared. Tables during this time were very close to the floor. The use of tall tables and chairs was uncommon. Dinner around the table would normally be accompanied by lounging on pillows and even bedlike areas for people to lie comfortably.

It was customary during that time when you entered a home for a servant to wash your feet. Imagine walking into a home and there being a servant standing nearby with a basin of water and a towel, waiting to clean your feet. It was necessary for one's feet to be washed once you entered a home, especially if you were going to eat at the low-lying tables where your feet would be within close proximity to the food. Foot washing was not a ceremonial custom, rather it was practically important because people walked in sandals or even barefoot through dusty, muddy, and waste-filled streets. During biblical days the sewer and trash systems existed in the forms of filling buckets and emptying them in to the streets, where the disciples walked everyday. Not surprisingly, washing someone else's feet was regarded as a demeaning task. It was normally reserved for a household servant. Evidently, no household servant was present at this meal.

When they entered the room, I imagine some of the disciples noticed that there wasn't a servant to wash their feet. I wonder if they lingered in the room waiting to be washed, or if they simply dismissed the apparent oversight. Eventually they chose to sit down at table. Jesus was about to do something shocking. Well, I wish it could be shocking to you, I wish it could startle you, but many of us have heard this story so much that...

> We lose the wonder of it.
> We lose the mystery of it.
> We lose the power of it.

Jesus removed his outer garment and wrapped a towel around his waist. His attire now resembled a household servant. In Luke 22, we find the same scene in the Upper Room, and it says a conversation arose among the disciples,

> Also a dispute arose among them as to which of them was considered to be the greatest. Jesus said to them, "The kings of Gentiles lord it over them; and those who exercise authority over them call themselves benefactors. But you are not to be like that. Instead, the greatest among you should be like the youngest, and the one who rules like the one who serves. For who is greater, the one who is at the table or the one who serves? Is it not the one who is at the

table? But I am among you as the one who serves. (Luke 22:24–27, NIV)

They sat at this table and argued about greatness, something they obviously know nothing about. Jesus had been with them three years, yet they still stumbled over the definitions of what it meant to become great. He had to show them.

With a towel around his waist, he poured water into a basin and moved towards the disciples to wash their dirty feet. It simply says, *"He began to wash his disciples feet."*

Can you imagine this moment? What were the disciples thinking? Were they thinking? Jesus then moved to the brash and bold Peter and he refused to let Jesus do this degrading act of service for him. Jesus looked at him and said, *"You will understand what I am doing later... unless I wash you, you have no part with me."* Once Jesus said this, Peter overreacted and responded by zealously asking for Jesus to wash all of him, but Jesus calmed Peter and only washed his feet, he encouraged him to let this lesson sink into his heart.

After he was finished washing their feet, he redefined leadership.

> When he had finished washing their feet, he put on his clothes and returned to his place. "Do you understand what I have done for you?" he asked them. "You call me 'Teacher' and 'Lord,' and rightly so, for that is what I am. Now that I, your Lord and Teacher, have washed your feet, you also should wash one another's feet. I have set you an example that you should do as I have done for you. I tell you the truth, no servant is greater than his master, nor is a messenger greater than the one who sent him. Now that you know these things, you will be blessed if you do them. (John 13:12–17, NIV).

Similar to what is read in Luke 22, Jesus defines greatness through servanthood. Greatness is synonymous with power. The disciples wanted to be considered powerful and great! Fresh in their memories were the palm branches that greeted Jesus, and I'm sure they felt like they we being honored along with Jesus as they entered Jerusalem. They were feeling significant, important, and powerful.

We all want to do something great. We hope to do something significant or something worth remembering. The problem isn't the desire to do something great or worth remembering. The problem is our understanding of greatness. The people who achieve what we define as greatness are those we admire, quote, and eventually try to *be like*. In the 1990s Gatorade had a popular ad campaign starring Michael Jordan. The campaign portrayed children everywhere trying to *be like Mike,* and the commercial had a catchy jingle repeating the words, "*I wanna be, I wanna be like Mike, like Mike, I'd like to be like Mike.*" I was just like the kids in that commercial. I too wanted to be like Mike. It might surprise you that I got very close to being like Mike, but in the end, I lacked a little thing called *talent.*

We are all different, yet we all want to be great.

This desire to be great leads people to become dangerously obsessed with the endeavor. Most of us are familiar with the fascinating magician/illusionist Harry Houdini, who performed in the early 1900s. He became famous for pioneering the art of escape, as displayed by readily escaping handcuffs, jails, straight-jackets, and even being buried alive. The most ironic thing about Houdini's life was what killed him. He wasn't killed by any of his most dangerous stunts, but he was killed as a *result* of those stunts.

Houdini had become prideful. He arrogantly claimed that he could withstand any blow to the body above his waist without injury. He invited any man tough enough to give him their best shot to prove his invincibility. A college student was willing to test his theory and punched Houdini in the gut three times when he wasn't ready to receive the blow. It's widely accepted that he had been suffering from appendicitis, and the punches caused his appendix to burst.[2] Although clearly in pain, he refused to receive medical attention and continued to perform and travel. He died a week later.

Proverbs says, "Pride comes before the fall."

We are surrounded by leadership that is full of pride. In this chapter, I've acknowledged our struggle with power, but I've also stated that power doesn't have to be bad. I've stated that doing something great is not the problem, but it's our understanding of greatness that can be the problem. When power and greatness are rooted in pride, it reeks of decay and selfish motive.

The disciples argued about greatness because they were disillusioned about themselves. They were giving themselves credit for what Jesus had done. They were becoming prideful. I witness pride in many people I encounter in leadership positions. I also realize that pride is a great challenge within my own life. Thinking too much of ourselves and giving ourselves too much credit is epidemic. Pride is exercised through the attention we give ourselves.

Quick test:

How much of your day is focused on you versus others?
How many of your prayers are focused on you versus others?
How much personal development is focused on you versus others?
How much of your conversations are related to you versus others?

Selfishness is the definition of pride. When we are selfish with our days, prayers, development, and conversations, we stink of pride.

We must ask ourselves, "What am I doing to *give it all away?*"

One of my mentors, Bo Boshers, shared this short phrase with me years ago by encouraging me to be a person that gives it all away. "Become a person who gives away words of encouragement, time, wisdom, resources, thoughts, and whatever you may have to serve others."

So again, perhaps leadership isn't even about leadership.

On the surface, leadership seems to be about having a position, having a contagious personality, being able to inspire others, dressing better than others, having a team of people to lead, creating expectations, and being smart. When I think about those things, I can easily become me-centered. They are things that I can take credit for. I can even create them through enough effort and then claim some sort of self-proclaimed leadership genius (I've seen it done).

Jesus is modeling a leadership style that has others in mind. Leadership that looks to empower others, bring the best out of people, draw people towards God's call in their lives, and become a person who is here not to *be* served, but to serve.

This requires humility.

So back to this *secondly* thing I mentioned earlier.

First, leadership is about courage.

Secondly, leadership is about humility.

Jesus turned the world on its head by embodying humility as the source and mark of greatness and power. He didn't just say to become humble, but he lived a life of complete service and humility, even to the point of death. Paul writes in the book of Philippians critical passages that inform us of the type of lives we must live.

> Do nothing out of selfish ambition or vain conceit. Rather, in humility value others above yourselves, not looking to your own interests but each of you to the interests of the others. In your relationships with one another, have the same mindset as Christ Jesus. Who, being in very nature God, did not consider equality with God something to be used to his own advantage; rather, he made himself nothing by taking the very nature of a servant, being made in human likeness. And being found in appearance as a man, he humbled himself by becoming obedient to death—even death on a cross! (Philippians 2:3–8, NIV)

The path Jesus chose to exemplify his power and greatness was not typical. He chose to descend from the top of creation seated on his throne with all *power*, and he entered our world and was spit on by his creation, beaten, and murdered. He was the King of kings, but he became a servant for the very least of these. His life violated all the world's definitions of leadership, greatness, and power, yet we read in Philippians 2:9, "Therefore God exalted him to the highest place and gave him the name that is above every name."

In his nothingness, he became everything! Paul then writes a thirty-four-word sentence in Philippians chapter three that is easy to skim over as *Bible talk* (You know, the stuff in the Bible that you consider too wordy or complicated to understand, so you read past it without much of a pause).

> I want to know Christ—yes, to know the power of his resurrection and participation in his sufferings, becoming like him in his death, and so, somehow, attaining to the resurrection from the dead. (Philippians 2:10–11, NIV)

What does it mean to know Christ and the *power of his resurrection*? In order to experience a resurrection, a death must occur. Obviously the resurrection of Jesus was preceded by his death. If we were going to assign power rankings to particular acts or miracles within Scripture, I'm sure the power to resurrect and overcome death would rank near the top, so it's no wonder Paul refers to it as the power he desires to experience and know. Paul describes throughout Philippians that becoming like Jesus and sharing his humility, obedience, and servant nature will usher in a power that is unlike any other power on this earth. It is a power that is unstoppable. This power isn't about achievement or position, but instead it's about *giving it all away*. It's a posture of servanthood and looking to become nothing in order to make Jesus everything.

Nothingness is not living a defeated and weak life and allowing the world to walk all over you. To become nothing, you initiate a heart to serve others with the hopes to make them better. You become a person who speaks life into others. You become the one who creates the culture around you by contagiously serving others. It is about building *His* kingdom, and it's never about building our *own* kingdom.

We often think power is an attitude of being willing to charge the hill. Maybe power is discovered in dying on that hill.

In order for *life* to be achieved (remember that's what this book is about—your life), death must occur. This is a basic principle of life. It is through the death of fruits, vegetables, and animals that you and I live. Unfortunately, Bessy the cow has to die in order to satisfy my carnivorous nature. "Moo, moo" and "cluck, cluck" just equates to dinner in my belly. If you eat you believe in the philosophy of death being the engine to life. Through death we receive physical life. In the same way, the death of our *old self* and its selfish, power-hungry ways is the engine *life to the full*.

Leadership is not about the type of leadership most of the world teaches us. It's not about climbing the organizational chart to fill the box that carries more positional authority. Leadership is about becoming a person who embodies certain characteristics and lives a certain way. Although the definitions of leadership will vary in our world, you can be clear about the definition you live. Jesus modeled a way that walks into the room and looks to serve others. He was singularly focused on bringing attention to God's kingdom to the people around him. He was willing to serve others that didn't respect him, believe him, or love him.

In today's culture, this can mean that we lead others by doing everything we can to help them with their hopes and dreams. We promote, encourage, and ultimately serve others in order to be a catalyst for the overall common good of our communities and all sorts of things that matter that we would have never thought of.

Leadership in this sort of perspective is less about you and more about *them*.

So many of us go through each day hoping someone will affirm us with a pat on the back, a phone call, or a reply to our social media update. May I suggest that instead of seeking affirmation, can we learn to *give* affirmation?

We all want to be valued and affirmed, and sadly, what I find is our desperation to receive affirmation limits our heart and vision to realize the potential to *give it away*.

Leading is about others, not you.

Darwin's law of the survival of the fittest has become the rules of engagement in a country that supports the philosophy of looking out for number one. Are we no more than animals? Eat or be eaten, really? What about being *for* others? What about being *for* the common good of our city, our community, and our friends?

I want you to imagine yourself as a leader who has enormous influence. Imagine being the type of leader who walks into the room and people hope to have conversation with you. Imagine being a leader who has the ability to create significant change.

Really, imagine this. Imagine that you are a great leader. For those of you who are arrogantly telling yourself that you are already great, go ahead and imagine that you are even greater.

Now imagine you are given two options—both options potentially lead to being this great level of leader. Both options require you to work hard, to intentionally develop yourself, to learn how to work well with others, and to initiate; however, both options also have some stark differences in focus and priority.

Option One:	Option Two:
1. Become driven about personal goals and dreams.	1. Become driven about being who God has called you to be.
2. Engage others in your vision.	2. Help others discover and live their dreams.

3. Always put yourself in the best light.

3. Shed light on the best qualities of others.

4. Seek promotion and advancement.

4. Always seek what is right.

5. Identify potential threats to your leadership.

5. Identify people you can join to serve good causes.

6. Dismiss people who get in the way.

6. Help those that others dismiss.

7. Partner with people that help you.

7. Help those that partner with you.

8. Invest in yourself.

8. Invest in others and yourself.

9. Dress the part.

9. Be yourself.

10. Surround yourself with people that make you better.

10. Surround yourself with people who you believe in.

11. Lead causes that others will respect.

11. Embody causes that matter.

12. Tirelessly pursue what you believe in.

12. Courageously pursue who God has called you to be.

Option one calls the individual to be committed and clear about what he or she wants. This is the typical path most choose and seems completely reasonable to a person with an agenda of climbing the ladder. Option two is an approach to simply being a humble and courageous person.

By the way both ways may result in you leading many people. But how do you want to lead? Who do you want to become?

Ultimately, leadership is not about leadership.

≈‽.⩗.⩕

Fears will prevent us from doing things that matter, and there will be times that we'll need to *kick fear in the face* and proclaim, "My God did not give me a spirit of fear, but one of *power*, love, and self-control."

Leadership is about having the courage to be humble in a world that isn't humble.

It's about having the courage to seek a different sort of power—one only accessed through servant-hood, goodness, and submission to the Father.

Leadership is not about gaining followers. That's why leadership isn't about leadership. Leadership begins with *following* Jesus and his countercultural ways of changing the world.

≈.♥.≈

Questions for Reflection And Conversation

1. How have you seen leadership defined and more importantly lived by the world around you? Good examples? Poor examples?

2. Has your courage ever been tested? How?

3. How has your own pride got in the way of your life and leadership?

4. How does Jesus example of leadership and humility in John 13 (and the rest of scripture) encourage you?

5. How does our leadership first being about following impact your life and thoughts about personal leadership?

CHAPTER NINE

Earthquakes and an Egyptian

I remember stepping out of the plane into the blazing sun on the tarmac instead of into an air-conditioned jet bridge, but it didn't matter because I was finally there. It was the summer of 2009 and for nearly three years I had been working with the Mission of Hope near Port-au-Prince, Haiti. I had sent a few mission teams prior to this trip, and I had planned on personally going on more than one occasion, but as life has it, circumstances had kept me from going until now. I had heard and learned so much about the country, but none of it had prepared me for what God was going to lead to me to experience.

I was leading a group of seventeen high school students and young adults, and it was everyone's first time to Haiti. It took all of the first hour in Haiti to realize that the statistics we had read were true. Haiti is the poorest country in the western hemisphere (the median age is only twenty years old). One out of every five children die before turning five years old, and well over 80 percent of the population live in abject poverty.[1] What we witnessed was well beyond third world.

My ten days in Haiti changed my view of the world. I held orphans, played soccer with children in the streets, painted a school, smelled their market, tasted their food, swam in their beautiful ocean (the water there is crystal blue), witnessed rampant unemployment, saw starvation, experienced their joy, saw their struggle, embraced their beauty, and sensed hope.

Haiti is thought to be hopeless by many. Its history is torn by political tyranny, voodoo curses, and oppression. The attempts for a better Haiti have always been thwarted by the immense hole the country finds itself in. There is a growing few in Haiti, some at the Mission of Hope, who are spreading the word that the hope of Haiti is not rooted in a political savior, but in the King of kings. The name of Jesus is growing in Haiti, and people are turning to him. We witnessed this on our trip.

As our trip neared its end, I gathered our team to reflect on what we had experienced and what the Lord was speaking to us about our time in Haiti. I gave everyone a rock that I had gathered from the area. I shared the story found in Joshua 4 when the Lord had the Israelites create a twelve-stone memorial to remember that the Lord had stopped the flow of the Jordan River at flood stage in order for Israelites to cross on dry ground. It was another miracle by the Lord, and this time he wanted to make sure they didn't *forget* as they had a habit of doing.

> Each of you is to take up a stone… to serve as a sign among you. In the future when your children ask you, 'What do these stones mean?' tell them that the flow of the Jordan was cut off before the ark of the covenant of the Lord. When it crossed the waters of the Jordan were cut off. These stones are to be a memorial to the people of Israel forever.(Joshua 4:5–7, NIV)

I passed out the rocks and asked the team to write with a marker on the stone a word or phrase that the Lord wanted them to remember. I invited them to seek the Lord about this and to receive a word from him. It was a beautiful experience together as we went around the circle and shared what God had spoken to us to remember. I led this time hoping it would provide a meaningful ending to our powerful ten days in Haiti. The word the Lord spoke to me; however, was not an ending, and it has had a profound impact on what God would do in the coming years. God led me to write two words.

"A Beginning."

The rock sits in my house on my bookshelf. I see it often and shake my head knowing how true that short statement has become.

That was in July of 2009 and in the coming months I discussed with my pastor of the church I served on staff with at the time (Journey Church in Norman, OK) to consider our philosophy concerning global missions, specifically how we choose our mission partners. We discussed options, which eventually led to the decision to take a giant step forward in choosing key strategic mission partners. In order to be a key mission partner, it was essential that our church recognized excellent leadership and a shared vision to potentially create tremendous transformation for the sake of Christ. In the initial review of all the organizations, we worked with around the world we felt the Mission of Hope fit best as our first key strategic partner.

Our church decided in the fall of 2009 to establish the Mission of Hope and the country of Haiti as our key mission partner and, therefore, the primary area of global mission emphasis. In order to communicate and share this vision with the church, our church created a short film about Haiti and the Mission of Hope. It was a powerful film exposing our church to the need that we could start serving. The film showed at our church in December 2009.

On January 12, 2010 a catastrophic earthquake hit the city of Port-au-Prince.

Do you ever have moments when you don't know what to do, but you know that something must be done? It's a moment you can't sit idly by.

Moses had such a moment.

ৡৢৣ

One day, after Moses had grown up, he went out to where his own people were and watched them at their hard labor. He saw and Egyptian beating a Hebrew, one of his own people. Looking this way and that and seeing no one, he killed the Egyptian and hid him in the sand. The next day he went out and saw two Hebrews fighting. He asked the one in the wrong, "Why are you hitting your fellow Hebrew?" The man said, "Who made you ruler and judge over us? Are you thinking of killing me as you killed the Egyptian?" Then Moses was afraid and thought, "What I did must have become known." When Pharaoh heard of this, he tried to kill Moses, but Moses fled... (Exodus 2:11–15, NIV)

Bill Hybels writes in his book, Holy Discontent, about this passage from Exodus being Moses's breaking point moment—it was the moment that he couldn't stand it any longer and he had to do something.[2]

We are much more familiar with the story after this moment in Moses's life. Moses runs and lives in hiding for decades. He's sure he will die an old man in obscurity, but God has other plans.

One day Moses is tending his flock and the Lord shows up in a burning bush and the story of the Exodus of God's people is born. We usually begin the story of the Exodus with the burning bush, but could this breaking point moment when Moses buried the Egyptian in the sand have been when things really began?

Moses is an Israelite (aka Hebrew); however, through miraculous circumstances he found himself living as an Egyptian and as part of Pharaoh's family. He hasn't experienced the slavery or the beatings that his fellow Hebrews had endured their entire lives. However, Moses knows that he is not an Egyptian; he is a Hebrew, and his people are being oppressed.

Imagine being a Hebrew slave and your entire day is spent making bricks and mortar—bricks to build elaborate Egyptian buildings (some of which still stand today) for the pleasure of Pharaoh, a man that claimed to be a god. Day after day you suffer in the Egyptian sun while slave drivers demand you meet your quota of bricks and work longer hours. This is what the Hebrew people are facing and Moses knows it, so he *"went out to where his own people were and watched them at their hard labor."* While watching, Moses witnesses an Egyptian beating a Hebrew, probably for not meeting his quota of bricks.

Moses couldn't quietly sit in the palace any longer.

He couldn't stand to see the oppression and the injustice, and he just snapped. The Scriptures say he *looked this way and that*, making sure no one was around, and he went to the defense of his countryman. It says he killed the Egyptian and buried him in the sand.

This crime made Moses a fugitive, and he fled Egypt. His actions were steeped in emotion and rage; however, his actions were also a response to injustice and oppression. Moses's encounter with the Egyptian was *his immature moment* of stating what ought to be different. His sense of duty to the injustice was right, but his actions were not. His decision to act irrationally delayed God's plan for another forty years. However, I think there is a reason God showed up in a burning bush years later and asked Moses to bring his people out Egypt. God found a man who cared about what he cared about. God saw the heart of Moses and *Moses cared about God's people*. God was looking for someone to care about what *should be* for his people.

So again I ask, do you ever have moments when you don't know what to do but you know something must be done?

In the coming days after January 12, 2010, we had no idea what to do, but we knew something had to do done. Our church was stirred to respond to this disaster in Haiti, and so was I. We determined that we could organize some medical teams to be sent to the Mission of Hope clinic, which had become a make-shift hospital.

The news of the aftermath of the earthquake was sobering. The shoddy construction, the widespread use of cinderblocks that you could crumble in your hands, and the congestion of people living on top of one another in the slums of Port-au-Prince had left the city with approximately 220,000 dead, over 300,000 wounded, and 1.5 million people homeless.

I headed up the organization of two medical teams to head out as soon as possible. We were told flights were not going into Haiti and that we would need to wait, but there was no time-table on when. We learned that our only option to get there quickly was to fly into the neighboring country of the Dominican Republic and to take the eight-hour bus ride to Port-au-Prince. We found our way in, so we packed our bags and headed to Haiti via the Dominican Republic.

We had a team of ten, which included my mom who went as one of the nurses. I was the only non-medical person on the team, so my role was to handle the logistics of getting in and out of Haiti (which was no small feat) and to serve throughout the trip however I could. We arrived in Haiti twenty days after the earthquake had hit. As we drew within a few miles of the mis-sion we drove past the mass gravesite that had been made since the earthquake. The bulldozers were still working to cover the approximate 150,000 people that were buried there. The damage was staggering.

Once we arrived at mission it was all business. Our medical team went to work helping people for sixteen plus hour shifts every day. They encountered countless amputees, infections, and the sickness in Haiti that existed prior to the earthquake. My role was challenging. I had never before felt so unneeded and out of place. In most circumstances I found myself in the position of leader, but what these people needed I didn't have the expertise to provide. Since I was white, Haitians often came to me for help, assuming I was a doctor, but I was *only* a pastor. I ended up doing a variety of things most notably assisting our paramedic, Curtis, who was handling the medical transfers in and out of the mission. The mission had recently been given an ambulance, which was clearly a result of God's provision for the mission during this time. Every day people came to the mission with medical needs too great to be handled on site, so they were transferred to the larger hospitals in Port-au-Prince.

This created experiences I will never forget. I remember helping Curtis carry a woman in a bed sheet who had died at the mission. Her family asked the mission if her body could be brought to their home. So we drove her to a nearby village in the middle of the night. When we stopped I opened the back door of the ambulance. The only lights in the village where the headlights of the ambulance; utter darkness continued to accompany every night since the earthquake. As I stepped out of the back of the ambulance, I encountered dozens of Haitian family and friends standing there silently and solemnly. Death of a loved one is sadly all too common for the people of Haiti—it always has been. We carried her from the ambulance and placed her in a shed of her family's small home. I was told they would bury her in the coming days.

The most powerful experience I witnessed had little to do with the earthquake but rather the plight in Haiti that preceded the earthquake and continues today. Two precious little boys ages eight and three showed up at the Mission of Hope clinic, and both had bloated tummies with swollen faces. They sat on the bed seemingly lifeless depleted of any energy. Even though they were eight and three, they looked more like four and one due to extreme malnourishment. It was a combination of not eating and eating the wrong thing. Their stomachs were full of *rocks*.

For years in Haiti "dirt cookies" have been something people have fed to children in the place of the lack food. They are intended to satisfy the desperate hunger pains by putting something in their stomachs. The cookie is what it sounds like. A cookie made of dirt with a little sugar or spice added to give some flavor. Their mother had nothing else to give them to satisfy their hunger. These two little boys were at a critical point, close to death. The doctors at the mission knew they needed dramatic medical attention, so they recommended they be taken to a hospital in Port-au-Prince.

Curtis, our driver, these two boys, their mother, and I set out to get them to the help they needed. Our first stop was the children's hospital at Port-au-Prince. We carried the boys in but were quickly turned away. The hospitals were overflowing from the aftermath of the earthquake and they claimed they couldn't help. We pleaded but to no avail. So we went to the next hospital and we found the same result and were finally told were told to try General. General Hospital is the downtown hospital located directly behind the Presidential Palace. The image of the destroyed Palace is what most people remember from the Haiti earthquake. We had been to General before and it was overrun with people, but the earthquake had brought the attention of the world, and it was no longer just General Hospital, but it was now the British Red Cross, the US Military, the United Nations, and countless other medical and government agencies that had set up dozens of tent hospitals all working together as one massive conglomerate.

We arrived at General and I remember carrying the older brother through the crowds of suffering people. On either side of us were crumbled buildings as we walked by tent after tent of endless beds of amputees and injured people. I couldn't believe he was eight. He was so light. He weighed less than my daughter at two years old. As I walked with him, I was overcome by his life. He was barely living, and once I left him at this hospital, I had no idea if anything would change. It wasn't right. It wasn't fair. All I could do was hope this moment would be the beginning of a new life for he and his brother.

It seemed like a long walk to that tent. We walked by twenty or thirty other tents until we found a tent almost as far as we could go that would finally take the boys. When we arrived I handed him to a nurse who quickly took him and began to take care of him. We turned around, walked back in the ambulance, and left.

There are times that something must be done.

I imagine that is how Peter felt the night that Judas showed up in the olive grove with a detachment of armed soldiers. Earlier that night, Judas had left dinner and went to the chief priests and Pharisees and handed Jesus over to them for thirty pieces of silver. Peter wasn't going to let this betrayal take place under his watch. Peter was brash and bold, and these accusers had no truthful basis for their charge against Jesus. Peter was carrying a sword just in case a moment like this ever happened. He drew his sword and acted before it was too late. He struck one of the high priest's servants and cut off his ear.

Can you imagine the scene? Jesus and his eleven disciples were not violent, but here they stood with one of Jesus's closest disciples holding the assault weapon in his hand.

Jesus immediately commanded, "Put your sword away!"

I'm sure Peter was ready to keep going, but he submitted to Jesus and dropped the sword. Scriptures say that Jesus touched the man's ear, and it was restored.

What? Jesus heals the man arresting him? Please tell me that man became one of his followers.

Peter responded to this moment with reactionary leadership. Reactionary leadership is dangerous. It doesn't consider the past or the future but only the present. When people simply react to moments out of emotion, other people get hurt. Emotional reactions are not what the world needs more of; however, Peter's passion to respond is something we all resonate with. He was stirred to action, and I'd rather be a person who is passionately stirred than one who sits on their hands and is never stirred to action about anything.

There are times that we must *do something*. This becomes our stirring. This becomes meat on the bone of that silent beckoning.

I and many others were stirred by the devastation in Haiti. Moses was stirred by the oppression of his people. What stirs you?

I've seen God use a promise on a rock to fan the flame of what could be. In the eighteen months after the earthquake, God used our church and other leadership measures I was able to be a part of to take hundreds of people to serve on short-term trips to Haiti, raise almost two hundred thousand dollars to help build a hospital, connect ministries and others churches from around the country to the Mission of Hope, provide leadership training for School of Hope kids (the MOH school), sponsor hundreds of kids to provide food and education, and I've seen young leaders (that I've gone to Haiti on a short-term trips with) pack up their lives and move to Haiti to serve as interns and staff members.

When we are stirred by something, that also stirs the heart of God, he will move.

If you ever say I can't take it anymore, or if you feel something must be done, well then, I have to ask you, *What are you gonna do about it?*

This isn't an invitation to go off the deep end like Moses or Peter (please, no dead Egyptians or severed ears). This is a call to do something that matters. This is a call to discover what stirs you. We all need something worth fighting for. Moses and Peter had been stirred. They were motivated by something that was good. We can't relate to their ancient experience of how they responded, but we can relate to the feeling of having to *do something*.

My experiences with Haiti have galvanized my stirring to become a person who dreams wildly, lives differently, loves, recklessly, and leads courageously.

You may be wondering, *What does Haiti has to do with that?*

Well, it has everything to do with it. Living a life where I aim to live the gospel out in such a way that doing things that matter in Haiti matters as much as my kids doing things that matter in their school. My time in Haiti has only softened my heart to the harsh realities of this world that the Christian community must do something about.

Christie and I want to fight for the betterment of the church. We, along with many of our friends at OKC Community Church, believe that the big "C" church can do better! That's why I wrote this book, and more importantly, that's why we have a belief that you and I can actually do things that matter for the kingdom every day.

What are the things that matter to you? What is a need that exists that you must do something about? How does it contribute to the mission of God and the good work he wants done in this world?

I'm not inviting or encouraging you to go off on some *religious rant,* where we act out of frustration to the broken world around us and end up pointing fingers at the things we wish were different. I'm inviting you to discover what stirs your soul from a place of compassion. A stirring that leaves you desiring to do something out of love, service, and the holy dissatisfaction that something must be done, no matter what it takes!

Think about every great leader the world has ever known. They are almost exclusively driven by great causes. *Great leaders are driven by great causes.* That sort of leadership isn't always popular or easy. Great leadership often comes at the price of being in a *lonely place.* Sometimes you'll have to stand on that limb all by yourself. Moses was alone, away from his countryman for decades before God showed up in a burning bush. Often when God stirs us it isn't going to be a popular movement.

On one occasion I remember a *leader* confidently telling me, "If you want to know if you're a leader, turn around and see if anyone is following."

At first take, it makes some sense. Leaders should have followers, but upon further reflection something smelled funky about that philosophy. In my mind's eye, I'd imagine who was behind me as I glanced over my shoulder, but I quickly realized that sometimes that mattered and sometimes it didn't. I wrestled with this because most people believe this. Most believe that the best leaders have the most followers, but what I'm discovering is that often the people who have the biggest "position" have the most followers. Meaning, whoever holds the more powerful position could easily maintain the larger following regardless of their actual leadership. As a result, people seek greater power and position so they can claim greater leadership, but few are stirred about something that matters. This is one reason why we have a nation full of unreached potential. Americans can change the world. We are positioned and resourced to serve our fellow brothers and sisters around the world but collectively, not enough of us have been stirred to do so.

We chase leadership in the form of greater esteem, larger titles, and bigger paychecks. We need leaders who are looking to be gripped by what stirs the heart of God and to faithfully and courageously give themselves to that cause.

Leadership is not about people following you.

Leadership is about you following God.

It's not about who is behind me when I turn around, but it's about who's ahead of me. If I am faithfully and courageously following God's stirring in my life, I can trust him with the outcomes of what will be.

Our world needs people *who can't take it anymore!*

- Who are not okay with their neighbors being nameless faces!

- Who are done with the walls of normalcy!

- Who are so over following prideful leadership!

- Who can't take the church's pineapple ways!

- Who are finished allowing fear to stop them!

- Who are tired of mediocre versions of faith!

Maybe you are in the place in life that Christie and I were in a few years ago (and in many ways has become a permanent place for us). A place of frustration and discontent, yet a desire for more and a sense that God was beckoning us! Something must be done in your life, and it is not okay to continue life as-is. God's Spirit is always on the move, we just need to start paying attention. For most of us our faith needs to get out of a seat, it needs to extend beyond quiet times, and it must come face to face with courageous decisions.

The conversation of this book has been about *your* life. Each step of the way we've explored a way of life that every one of us can live, but as Jesus said in Matthew 7, "It will not be an easy endeavor."

In many ways, it requires a faith beyond reason. That sort of faith requires extreme measures of courage. Faith and courage are intrinsically linked. You cannot be faithful without being courageous. Faith will always be accompanied by moments of courage to do the right thing, to trust God with the scary thing, and to step into the places you thought you'd never go.

The life God has for us is beyond our comprehension and imagination. Paul speaks of this in 1 Corinthians 2, when he writes, "No mind can imagine what God has in prepared for those who love him." For years I said, "I'd never plant a church."

I've always believed in church planting, but I thought it just wasn't for me. I also said I'd never have a minivan, yet Christie and I are now rocking the mini on date nights. (I hate that minivans are just so darn practical!). So maybe the lesson is *never say never*? Perhaps, but more likely the lesson is God has more in you than you'll ever realize. And if you'll *faithfully* respond to that stirring within you, you'll find yourself doing all sorts of things you never saw coming.

> The gospel will lead you
> to do things you thought
> you'd never do.
> The gospel will lead you
> to do things you never knew
> you wanted to do.

What stirs you?

The founders of the Mission of Hope Haiti, Brad and Vanessa Johnson, were first stirred to help those in Haiti by handing out pieces of bread with peanut butter in order to provide kids with needed protein and nourishment. The story has gone well beyond peanut butter.

As of 2014, they have an orphanage of over 65 kids aimed at raising up the next generation of leaders in Haiti, their schools house over 7,700 students from kindergarten through twelfth grade and provide them a Christian education, they feed over 97,000 meals everyday through their feeding program, they provide thousands of people health care through their hospital, they host hundreds of people in mission teams *every week*, they provide hundreds of jobs for Haitians, they are building and giving away hundreds of homes to Haitian families, they have a large vibrant church that serves the surrounding communities, they are working to advance and plant churches around the entire nation, and they provide a host of other influences to the country of Haiti in their attempts to point people to the hope that is found in Jesus Christ.

The earthquake only created greater avenues and opportunity for the mission to be the city on the hill that is shining God's light of hope in the face of a nation in darkness. The Mission of Hope began with a stirring.

God has something he cares about that he wants you to care about too. It could be anywhere or anything, but it's out there, and it needs you.

What stirs you?

Now is the time to lead courageously and respond to that stirring by *doing things that matter.*

೩.♥.೬

Questions for Reflection And Conversation

1. What stood out for you from the story of Moses's actions with the Egyptian? What can we learn about what to do and what not to do in leadership?

2. How do you identify with the statement *leadership can be a lonely place*?

3. Reflect and write about three things that stir you.

4. What are some tangible steps you could take towards doing things that matter with what stirs you? (i.e., conversations with new people, prayer, research, etc...)

CHAPTER TEN

Stories That Matter

L iving a life that matters must be full of actually doing all sorts of things that matter. Doing things that matter doesn't mean you have to create your own huge, global-spanning movement. No. Instead it's contributing to the largest, global-spanning movement in the history of the world. Finding ways to live and be the person that God has created you to be. This is not about following religious rules or law. This is about love. This is about loving God, loving life, loving others, and as a result, having a life that you actually choose to live.

This journey for Christie and I started with a story. A story of telling our kids each morning as I dropped them off at school to do things that matter. It's funny how when you begin saying something like that and open yourself up to actually *doing things that matter* you'll actually find yourself living a life that is full of *life*. To this day, we encourage our kids everyday with this. We pray we will be a family that lives this way. We even have these words hanging over our door so when we leave our home and head into our life beyond our family, we never forget that our life matters, the people we'll see that day matter, and our words, actions, and decisions matter.

Our family often talks at dinner about the simple things that God is doing in us and the ways he's led us to do something that we know matters. Christie and I love hearing stories from our kids. Addi, our youngest daughter, often tells us stories. As a kindergartener, she shared a story of how she asked a friend if she could pray for her friend's "owie" after she fell and scraped her knee. Another time she gave her bracelet to a friend that simply liked her bracelet, and she has told us how she tries to help the kids that are new or don't have a lot of friends.

Doing things that matter won't happen by accident. They happen on purpose. Your life's story isn't something that will occur on accident. Your story will become exactly what your lead it to become.

If you want to have a life of watching TV and eating Cheetos, that will be your story. If you want give your heart to anger, regret, or unforgiveness, that will be your story. If you want to give the best of yourself to chasing more money, that will be your story. If you want to obsess over sports for your kids or yourself, that will be your story. If you want to cling to security measures that keep you grounded in the sea of sameness, that will be your story.

But if you become a person who has a *life full* of doing things that matter then that will be your story. You only have one life to live, and no one is responsible for it but you. He calls us out of the mundane and mediocre. He beckons us to experience life to the full.

> For most of us,
> the danger is not that we'll become *bad* people
> who don't care about things that *matter*.
> No, the danger is that we become *good* people
> who don't actually *do* anything that matters.

It is through Jesus that you can fearlessly *make the cannonball into the pool of uncertainties, questions, and endless possibilities* that your story with Christ has in front of you. I encourage you to live intentionally and remember that following Jesus will be an unpredictable, powerful, always moving, painful, joyful, purposeful, desperate, intentional, humble, exuberant, courageous, and overwhelming existence every day of your life.

Experiencing John 10:10's *superabundance of life* is a choice to keep going, push further, climb higher, and endure longer. It's accepting the invitation of the silent beckoning that God whispers to us inviting us deeper. Pursue *the journey of becoming who God has created you to be* more relentlessly than those crazies who risk their lives pursuing the thrill of standing on top of Mt. Everest. Become a believer that no matter what is sacrificed, risked, or endured along the way that it is worth every step. Dedication to a journey like that will change a life…it can change the world.

What if you allowed the seemingly impossible to become possible?

What if everyday you made choices that caused you to live differently?

What if you loved God and others with reckless abandon and a selfless heart?

What if you never allowed fear to stop you?

If you pursue the journey to dream wildly, live differently, love recklessly, and lead courageously all for the glory of God you will discover a life that is well lived. Don't just do something— *become someone.*

> Wake up every day and choose to be who God has called you to be.

This has been a book about life. More specifically, it's been about *your life.* May you become a person who lives a life full of stories that matter. I leave you with Paul's prayer for the Church of Thessalonica—this is my prayer for you.

> With this in mind, we constantly pray for you, that our God may count you worthy of his calling, and that by His power He may bring to fruition your every desire for goodness and your every deed prompted by faith. We pray this so that the name of our Lord Jesus may be glorified in you, and you in him, according to the grace of our God and the Lord Jesus Christ (2 Thessalonians 1:11–12, NIV).

NOTES

CHAPTER ONE
The Silent Beckoning

1. Grylls, Bear. Mud, Sweat, And Tears: The Autobiography. New York, NY: Harper Collins Publishers, 2012.

2. Barclay, William. The Daily Study Bible: Gospel of John. Vol. II. Louisville, KN: Westminster, John Knox Press, 2001.

CHAPTER TWO
Becoming a Dreamer

1. Batterson, Mark. The Circle Maker: Praying Circles Around Your Biggest Dreams and Greatest Fears. Grand Rapids, MI: Zondervan, 2011.

CHAPTER THREE
Scale the Walls of Normalcy

1. "Martin Luther King I Have a Dream Speech–American Rhetoric." Martin Luther King I Have a Dream Speech–American Rhetoric. http://www.americanrhetoric.com/speeches/mlkihaveadream.htm.

2. www.worldvoyageur.com/great-quotes/helen-keller-collected-quotations/.

CHAPTER FOUR
Living the Gospel

1. "Apologetics Press." Apologetics Press. http://www.apologet-icspress.org/APContent.aspx?category=11&article=1272.

CHAPTER FIVE
The Church Doesn't Matter

1. en.wikipedia.org/wiki/Postmodernity
2. Kinnaman, David and Gabe Lyons. Unchristian: What a New Generation Really Thinks About Christianity...And Why It Matters. Grand Rapids, MI: Baker Books, 2007.

CHAPTER SIX
Human Good

1. Ortberg, John. Who Is My Neighbor. Sermon at Menlo Presbyterian Church, November 2013.

CHAPTER SEVEN
Neighbors

1. McManus, Erwin. Chasing Daylight: Seizing the Power of Every Moment. Nashville, TN: Thomas Nelson Inc., 2002.
2. Pathak, Jay and Dave Runyon. Art of Neighboring: Building Genuine Relationships Right Outside Your Door. Grand Rapids, MI: Baker Books, 2012.

CHAPTER EIGHT
Leading Isn't about Leading

1. Pathak, Jay and Dave Runyon. Art of Neighboring: Building Genuine Relationships Right Outside Your Door. Grand Rapids, MI: Baker Books, 2012.
2. Forbes. http://www.forbes.com/wealth/powerful-people#p_1_s_arank.

CHAPTER NINE
Earthquakes and an Egyptian

1. "The Death of Houdini." Harry Houdini -. http://www. thegreatharryhoudini.com/death.html.

2. "Help Us Provide Prosthetic Care to 240 More Haitians!" Haiti Facts: Information About Haiti & Haiti Now. http:// www.mohhaiti.org/about_moh/haiti_info/.

3. Hybels, Bill. Holy Discontent: Fueling the Fire that Ignites Personal Vision. Grand Rapids, MI: Zondervan, 2007.

ONE LAST BIT ON THE AUTHOR
AND A FEW OTHER GREAT THINGS

Tim Mannin is a pastor and church planter. In 2012 he and his wife Christie started OKC Community Church. Located in the heart of Oklahoma City, their church aims to help people experience the love of Jesus and His gift of *life to the full*. Tim also writes and coaches for LEAD222, an international coaching network of church leaders. Tim and Christie are living the dream along with their four children, Emily, Carys, Addison, and Greyson.

Speaker & Questions

Tim is a passionate, genuine, and creative communicator. If you would like to contact Tim about an opportunity to speak at an event or your church, or if you have any questions, please go to www.doingthingsthatmatter.com or you can contact him directly through his church at info@okccommunitychurch.com.

OKC Community Church is a group of people who desire to be the church the best way they know how. They are working and dreaming to bring life to a city in an ever-changing culture where the church must learn new ways to share the story of God. For more on their story go to www.okccommunitychurch.com

LEAD222 is an international coaching and mentoring
organization aimed at serving ministry
leaders and student ministries.
www.lead222.com

hazel

PAPER CO.

Huge thanks to my talented friend Leslie
Koch, for designing the book cover.
Check out her amazing design company
at www.hazelpaperco.com

Made in the USA
Middletown, DE
16 August 2018